SECRET PLAYBOOK

SECRET PLAYBOOK

21 PLAYS TO UNLOCK THE SECRETS TO A PURPOSEFUL LIFE

WRITTEN BY NFL GREAT
FRANK D. MURPHY
FROM THE JAIL CELL TO THE NFL

FOREWORD BY COACH LOU HOLTZ

301 W Platt St A#221
Tampa Fl 33606

Secret Playbook
By Frank D. Murphy Jr.

Printed in the United States of America.

First edition: 2024
10 9 8 7 6 5 4 3 2 1

ISBN: 979-8-9914218-1-2 (Paperback)

This guide was designed and developed by Frank D. Murphy Programs (www.frankdmurphy.com) and ReEntry Institute (www.ReEntryInstitute.com).

FOREWORD

Greetings!

This is Coach Lou Holtz.

I have seen Frank D Murphy speak in person and he really encourages and motivates others with his life story. Frank is the type of young man that could have played on my team. His message shares the secrets of how to live a purposeful life and he also reveals how he became successful, and most importantly how he overcame adversity. This makes this book a must read.

There was no secret to how I coached my team to win the 1988 National Championship. It took the right attitude and the willingness to put in the hard work. That's exactly what my friend Frank D Murphy did when he wrote the Secret Play Book.

He wrote this book with the right attitude and put in the hard work to show others how they can become successful by following these 21 plays. By reading and following these secret plays you will be ready to take on your next challenge and accomplish your next goal. Remember you were born a winner. You were not born a loser. You are what you believe you can be. This book will help you to not give up but push you to new heights, no matter if it's in sports, in the classroom or in business.

Thank you, Frank, for all you do for the community and beyond. Like I always say, don't be a spectator. Don't let life pass you by. Frank's secret plays are your playbook for success.

Lou Holtz is an American former football coach and analyst. He served as the head football coach at the College of William & Mary, North Carolina State University, the New York Jets, the University of Arkansas, the University of Minnesota, the University of Notre Dame, and the University of South Carolina, compiling a career college head coaching record of 249–132–7. Holtz's 1988 Notre Dame team went 12–0 with a victory in the Fiesta Bowl and was the consensus national champion. Holtz is the only college football coach to lead six different programs to bowl games and the only coach to guide four different programs to the final top 20 rankings. After retiring from coaching, Holtz worked as a TV college football analyst for CBS Sports in the 1990s and ESPN from 2005 until 2015. On May 1, 2008, Holtz was elected to the College Football Hall of Fame.

Secret Playbook

Based on Frank D. Murphy's Journey From the Jail Cell to the NFL

ABOUT

The *Secret Playbook* is a self-guided workbook that unlocks the secrets to a purposeful life — play by play. Its author, Frank D. Murphy, former NFL player and national motivational speaker, uses his personal journey to help the reader take an in-depth look at their life and their journey to a purposeful life. Each secret play provides wisdom and practices that are lifechanging. Frank also shares examples of his own life experiences to inspire readers to get out of their own way and seek out their life purpose. This self-guided workbook is a tool that will help the reader see they have the ability to rewrite their future and let go of old habits and practices. Readers will learn they can create any life they want no matter how difficult it may seem; they will learn to identify and overcome obstacles; and most importantly, they will learn to live life with a purpose meant to help others. This guide is a useful training tool for communities, organizations, and educational as well as justice involved institutions who are exploring the implementation or enhancement of a current program to teach life skills and to divert individuals from the criminal justice system.

Secret Playbook

Based on Frank D. Murphy's Journey From the Jail Cell to the NFL

ABOUT

The *Secret Playbook* is a self-guided workbook that unlocks the secrets to a purposeful life — play by play. Its author, Frank D. Murphy, former NFL player and national motivational speaker, uses his personal journey to help the reader take an in-depth look at their life and their journey to a purposeful life. Each secret play provides wisdom and practices that are lifechanging. Frank also shares examples of his own life experiences to inspire readers to get out of their own way and seek out their life purpose. This self-guided workbook is a tool that will help the reader see they have the ability to rewrite their future and let go of old habits and practices. Readers will learn they can create any life they want no matter how difficult it may seem; they will learn to identify and overcome obstacles; and most importantly, they will learn to live life with a purpose meant to help others. This guide is a useful training tool for communities, organizations, and educational as well as justice involved institutions who are exploring the implementation or enhancement of a current program to teach life skills and to divert individuals from the criminal justice system.

TABLE OF CONTENTS

A MESSAGE FROM FRANK D. MURPHY

Dear Friend,

I would like to personally congratulate you for taking the first steps to unlock the secrets to a purposeful life. I assure you the *Secret Playbook* will take you on a journey that will cause you to ***Reflect*** on your past and how you're currently living your life; ***Refocus*** your thoughts and change your behavior; and ***Respond*** by taking the necessary actions towards pursuing your goals and living a productive life. I'm excited you have decided to embark on this journey with me. Once you've completed this course, I'm confident you will have all the tools necessary to take major steps toward reaching your full potential and your life's purpose.

The *Secret Playbook* is your personal tool for jotting down your thoughts, goals, and plans. It is filled with exercises which will later serve as a personal-development resource full of your personal reflections. My journey has provided me with vital secret plays that I'm excited to share with you. I'm confident that my real-life stories ("Frank's Story"), "Frank's Challenges", and the "Time Out" lessons will provide you with the vital tools, steps and lessons you need for success.

I encourage you to tackle this course immediately – you won't regret it. This course will require some light reading and a lot of self-reflection however I know you're up for the challenge. Thank you for allowing me to be part of your journey.

Regards,

Frank D. Murphy
Founder/CEO
Frank D. Murphy Program/Mentor With Purpose Charity

Believe It, Claim It, and Work It Out…

HOW TO USE YOUR PLAYBOOK

To get started, first you need to understand what a playbook is. A playbook is a book containing strategies, tactics, and methods that can be used for a team (or individual) to be successful. A playbook is comprised of specific plays. A play is a designed and practiced set of actions created to help you score points and win the game. The flow of the game will put you in situations where you will use a specific play from your playbook to better your opportunity to succeed in the game. The team that studies and follows the playbook the most effectively will win the game.

In this workbook, we have taken the concept of the playbook and applied it to life. Now it is very important you understand that first and foremost, you must be playing with the correct playbook, and you have to know how and when to utilize the correct plays. Which playbook are you currently using? Is it a playbook that enables you to participate and be successful in the game of life? When the flow of the game (your life) puts you in different situations, how will you use your playbook? Have you created the right plays, so that in any scenario life brings, you will be in the best situation to succeed?

The *Secret Playbook* encompasses plays you need to study to ensure success, as well as advice and techniques on how to build the right playbook for your life. To build the right playbook, you must understand the experiences that caused you to create the wrong playbook for your life in the first place. Once you understand these experiences, then you can confidently create a new playbook.

You should read and study your Playbook regularly. Remember practice makes perfect. You must study the workbook and complete all of its exercises and challenges in order to become stronger and compete at the top of your game. As you study the Playbook and complete the exercises, you will gain clarity, skills, and knowledge. Make sure you return to the Plays as often as necessary. Repetition helps us to retain and learn new information.

GETTING STARTED

Each play begins with the title of the Secret Play and an introduction. Reading this information will help you understand how the play is meant to be applied to your life. The introduction is followed by **_Frank's Story_**. These short stories are Frank's real-life experiences, and it gives you a look into Frank's personal journey and highlights how he used the Secret Plays in his life. After Frank's Story you will find sections entitled **_Reflect, Refocus_**, and **_Respond_**. In these sections your asked to sit back and **_Reflect_** on how the play relates to your life; **_Refocus_** your thoughts and behaviors of your old playbook so that you remove the mistakes that your old playbook allowed you to make; and **_Respond_** – go out and DO IT! Take your time answering the questions in these sections and be sure you are giving the most honest and complete answers you can. When you have completed the exercise, think about what you learned and put it into practice.

Throughout your workbook, you will see **_Frank's Challenges_** in which Frank himself challenges you to take steps to master the Secret Play. You'll also see **_Time Out's_** where Frank shares nuggets of information and wisdom with you that you will find relevant to the play you're studying.

Remember, the game is your **life**, and you are the player. It's your responsibility to ensure you are armed with the right plays and playbook in order to win the game. We challenge you to start building your new playbook today. What are you waiting for?

EMPTY YOUR CUP FOR THE SECRET PLAY

In order to move on from the past, you must empty your cup. You must empty all of your past negative experiences. Empty your hurt, struggles, even the names that people call you. If you don't empty your cup, you can't receive something new because your cup is already full of speculations, opinions, and bad experiences. If you want to change your life, you must empty your cup so that truth, encouragement, wisdom, love, and motivation can be put inside of your cup so that you can see the light of day.

FRANK'S STORY

When I went to jail at the age of 15, I walked in, and I smelt the stench of filthy socks. I noticed the paint chipping off the walls. When I walked into my cell, I realized that this was not the place for me and the people that were in there were not like me. As I sat there and heard other inmates talk and saw how other inmates interacted, I knew this wasn't the place for me and I had to find out what I was full of. What within myself did I have to empty out so that I would never be incarcerated like this again. When I heard the bars close behind me, that was the start of me emptying my cup.

I had to start reflecting on my bad decisions and how I ended up in this situation. Whatever you went through in life that brought you to the point you are in today, you must release those experiences and empty your cup. Emptying your cup is difficult because sometimes you don't even realize how much the past affects you. It's not easy to recognize the pain you may still feel from past experiences, because you may not even be aware that your past experiences are the cause of your current pain.

There may be things that happened in the past that you have yet to forgive yourself for. Or maybe not enough time has passed for you to get over something or someone. Try to examine how the past has affected you. When you do this, it will cause you to self-reflect. Go back to the moments that have completely changed the course of your life and reflect on those moments. That moment for me was when I sat in that jail cell at the age of 15. When was that moment for you? Write it down.

REFLECT

Think about it.

What are you struggling to empty out of your cup? *Is it a past relationship, a family member you need to distance yourself from, a bad decision you have made? Etc.*

How is the past impacting the choices you are currently making and will make in the future?
Are you currently keeping a person in the "friend zone" because you are afraid of being hurt as you were in a past relationship? Are you second-guessing college because of a negative experience you had in high school?

FRANK'S CHALLENGE 	Think back on your past experiences. Forgive that person or persons who mistreated you. Do not use those past experiences as a shield to not begin new relationships or experience new experiences. Instead, use the mistakes made from previous relationships and experiences as a reminder of how not to be treated in your new relationships and what not to do in new experiences.

Now it is time to refocus. Change your thought pattern so that you can begin to let go of the past. You will never forget the past, however you can't allow the past to alter your future. It's a process. It won't happen overnight, however every day that you take a step in the right direction you are making progress.

Refocus your Mind.

Now that you know what it is that you need to empty out of your cup, how will you make these changes? *If you are holding on to a past relationship, what steps will you take to move on from that experience and live a healthy life? Write down those steps.*

TIME OUT WITH FRANK D. MUR-PHY: After writing down the changes that you need to make to empty your cup, rank your changes from most urgent to least urgent. Begin working on these changes from most urgent to least urgent until every change is made.

Spend time doing the things that make you happy and with people who make you happy. After emptying your cup of all your negative experiences, it's time to begin your journey of refilling your cup. New experiences and spending time with people who make you happy is a good way of refilling your cup in a positive way.

Take action right **NOW!**

Are you spending time with the people who make you happy? *If you said no, then it is time for you to find a new circle of friends to spend time with.*

☐ **Yes**   ☐ **No**

Have you forgiven the ones who hurt you? *Give yourself permission to forgive. While emptying your cup, it is okay to forgive the ones who hurt you, although you have given yourself space to move on.*

☐ **Yes**   ☐ **No**

FRANK'S CHALLENGE

Write down the names of the people or things that hurt you on a blank sheet of paper. Once you write them down, draw a big "X" through the paper, ball it up, throw it away and let it go. Every time these people or things try to come back in your life and bother you, redo it again.

PLAY 1 WRAP UP

It's hard to let go of the past. To let go, you must make the decision to take control of your situation, but this may take time. Give yourself time to refocus on how you see your past situations and celebrate small victories. If you do this successfully, you will start to see your cup empty. Do you believe that you deserve to get off the bench and get back in the game?

☐ **Yes**   ☐ **No**

WHAT'S YOUR PLAN TO MASTER PLAY 1? Write it down!

Are you spending time with the people who make you happy? *If you said no, then it is time for you to find a new circle of friends to spend time with.*

☐ **Yes**　　☐ **No**

Have you forgiven the ones who hurt you? *Give yourself permission to forgive. While emptying your cup, it is okay to forgive the ones who hurt you, although you have given yourself space to move on.*

☐ **Yes**　　☐ **No**

FRANK'S CHALLENGE

Write down the names of the people or things that hurt you on a blank sheet of paper. Once you write them down, draw a big "X" through the paper, ball it up, throw it away and let it go. Every time these people or things try to come back in your life and bother you, redo it again.

PLAY 1 WRAP UP

It's hard to let go of the past. To let go, you must make the decision to take control of your situation, but this may take time. Give yourself time to refocus on how you see your past situations and celebrate small victories. If you do this successfully, you will start to see your cup empty. Do you believe that you deserve to get off the bench and get back in the game?

☐ **Yes**　　☐ **No**

WHAT'S YOUR PLAN TO MASTER PLAY 1? Write it down!

Now it is time to refocus. Change your thought pattern so that you can begin to let go of the past. You will never forget the past, however you can't allow the past to alter your future. It's a process. It won't happen overnight, however every day that you take a step in the right direction you are making progress.

Refocus your Mind.

Now that you know what it is that you need to empty out of your cup, how will you make these changes? *If you are holding on to a past relationship, what steps will you take to move on from that experience and live a healthy life? Write down those steps.*

TIME OUT WITH FRANK D. MURPHY: After writing down the changes that you need to make to empty your cup, rank your changes from most urgent to least urgent. Begin working on these changes from most urgent to least urgent until every change is made.

Spend time doing the things that make you happy and with people who make you happy. After emptying your cup of all your negative experiences, it's time to begin your journey of refilling your cup. New experiences and spending time with people who make you happy is a good way of refilling your cup in a positive way.

Take action right **NOW!**

POSITION YOURSELF FOR THE SECRET PLAY

Put yourself in the right position to be successful. Success requires a certain position and a certain location. For example. If you are seeking to become a great basketball player, you will not go to a football training coach. Or if you are looking to go to Atlanta, Georgia, and you head South from Orlando, Florida, you will never get to Georgia.

"To be successful, you must be going in the right direction" (quote from Pastor Greg Powe). No matter how good your car looks, no matter how much gas you have, if you are trying to get to Georgia from Florida, you will never get there if you go south. No matter how many times you pray, no matter how many times you jump around, no matter how many people you call, you have to be going in the right direction to get to the right position and location to be successful.

Mark 11:24 says, "You can pray for anything, and if you believe that you've received it, it will be yours." Prayer plays a huge role in positioning yourself for success. When you are praying and preparing, God is positioning you for success behind-the-scenes. You must believe that there is something bigger than you, working on your behalf. But you also have to know that you have a part to play in your success. Do you believe that you must play a part as well? What parts do you believe you have to play to be successful?

I had an opportunity to make it to the NFL, but I had to play a part. I had to study my playbook, I had to lift weights, I had to run, I had to eat right. The NFL gave me an opportunity, but just because you are given an opportunity doesn't mean that you will be successful. An opportunity gives you a chance to be successful, but you must play your part. Think about some of the things that you are trying to be successful at. Are you positioned to do those things? If not, what are you waiting for?

FRANK'S STORY

I will never forget Peyton Manning called me one day, when I was working for D1 Training Chattanooga. Manning was the owner and he called me in the offseason to ask if I could run routes and catch footballs for him. He asked if I was in shape because he was bringing another quarterback to throw with him. I said, "yea I'm in shape." When I got to the football field in a private location, it was him and Tom Brady.

I thought to myself "What! I'm about to catch for two of the best quarterbacks who ever lived." So, I warmed up and I started to run routes. I will never forget what Peyton said to me. He said, "Frank, if you run right to that spot, not too far left, not too far right, not too far deep, but right there, I will get you the ball every time. Every time I was in the right position, I caught the ball, and the ball was on time and on the money. Tom was a little different. He just said to be in the area, and I will get the ball to you.

I started to understand that if you are in the right position for success, you are going to get the right results every time. If you are in the wrong position the ball will go left, go right, or fall to the ground. This experience helped me realize that it is just as important to be in the right position, then it is to just know what you are supposed to be doing because you can know what you are supposed to be doing but could be out of position and you still miss your opportunity. A lot of people are missing their blessings and missing their rewards because they are out of position.

One of the biggest secrets to success is knowing how to put yourself in position to be successful. If you want to be successful, you must do things that will line up your purpose and position perfectly to bring success into your life. You can miss out on opportunities if you put yourself in the wrong position. To find success, there is a certain position that you are supposed to be in.

Are you in the right position to be successful? If not, then maybe you are headed in the wrong direction. What do you need to change to be in the right position? For example, are there any friends you need to leave behind, any habits you need to break? If you want to be in a career that requires training, are you doing everything in your power to get that training? Are you surrounding yourself with people who are masters in the craft you desire to obtain? Think about it.

REFLECT

Think about it.

What does success look like for you? *Is it money to you? Is it showing off in front of friends to you? This is not what success should look like. You must know what success looks like in order to be in the right position to achieve it.*

Are you taking the right steps to be in a place for success?

☐ **Yes**   ☐ **No**

TIME OUT WITH FRANK D. MUR-PHY: A position is not for you to lord over others. It's for you to serve others and lead them to a safe place.

What can you do to put yourself in a better position to be successful? *Can you make better decisions? What about not going along with the crowd and doing what the rest of society does? You have to know what works best for you.*

TIME OUT WITH FRANK D. MUR-PHY: You must be afraid of repeated failure in the same area.

Do not be afraid of failure because failure will happen to all successful people. You cannot make the same mistakes over and over and expect different results.

Think outside of the box. Thinking outside of the box helps you aim higher and creates a bigger vision than what you had before. Do not be afraid to follow your intuition. Your intuition is that little voice on the inside of you that tells you stop, go, yes, or no.

Refocus your Mind.

FRANK'S CHALLENGE

You must pay attention to that voice. That voice will take you down a path that will help you avoid unnecessary problems on your journey to success. I call this voice the HOLY SPIRIT. We all have it, so don't ignore it. This is not something that is spooky. It is a small still voice that leads you in the right direction and encourages you to make the right decisions.

Are you afraid of failure? *It's not unusual to be afraid of failure, but you must get past being afraid. Failure is a learning experience and can be a crucial part of your success.*

☐ **Yes**   ☐ **No**

In what ways can you think outside the box?

TIME OUT WITH FRANK D. MURPHY: When you position yourself, it will not be comfortable. It's designed to stretch your faith and will help you for the next position you are moving into.

Be willing to put in the work. You have to be willing to put in the work because if you don't, someone else will. Remember, hard work always pays off in the end. Talent will get you through the door, but **hard work and character** will keep you in the room. If you only spend 30 minutes a day working on your goals to be successful those 30 minutes add up. Calculate what 30 minutes a day adds up to in a week, a month, or a year. That's the amount of time you put into working towards being successful.

RESPOND!

Take action right **NOW!**

Are you willing to put in the work? *Be a person of action, not procrastination. It's Your Time!*

☐ **Yes**   ☐ **No**

PLAY 2 WRAP UP

Through prayer and meditation time, ask God what is needed from you to help position yourself to live a successful life.

WHAT'S YOUR PLAN TO MASTER PLAY 2? Write it down!

BUILDING YOUR PLATFORM FOR THE SECRET PLAY

What is a platform? A platform is something that you stand on. When it comes to your platform, what platform are you standing on? You should be standing on your moral values, character, integrity, and standards. Your platform is something that holds you up and that you can stand by.

What are some of the things that you should disconnect from that are killing your platform? For example, partying more than you work. Something like that will kill your platform. Not knowing when to let go of old friends on your new platform. What is it that you need to disconnect from?

What are some of the things that are stopping others from connecting to you on your platform? For example, is it because you tell lies? Is it because you cheat people? Is it because you always have excuses? Is it because you are finessing others? What are those things for you?

Your platform is not just your talent. Your platform is many things. Talent will create a platform, but character will help you maintain your platform to build your legacy. Your platform is not all about you. Your platform is not just for your family members or your friends. Are you building a platform only for your family and friends? If you answer yes, then you are missing the purpose of having a platform. Your platform will build a legacy for all. Not just your generation, but all generations to come. If you create your platform to help your family and friends, then you missed the whole purpose of what it's for.

A legacy completes your life's work as something that benefits future generations. It's a drive to create something greater than yourself, something that forever improves the world. How will you create a legacy for others? Will it be a book? Will it be a non-profit organization?

Even if you are a hairstylist, you can encourage people every day who come and sit in your chair. This will create a legacy and impact people as well. How will you use your talents and skills to help build your platform? Are you a singer, writer, athlete, educator?

Building a platform and creating a legacy doesn't happen overnight. But if you find your true purpose, and create your legacy with hard work and dedication, you can leave a mark on this world that will be forever celebrated by others.

TIME OUT WITH FRANK D. MUR-PHY: Character is making the right decisions when no one is watching. What you do in the dark will come out in the light. Integrity means in any situation, you are still honest, and use strong morals to win instead of being dishonest.

FRANK'S STORY

Being in the NFL, I had to find somebody to look up to, who had character and integrity. When you go into the NFL, most people are just partying, kicking it, sleeping with a lot of women, and just doing their thing. But I began to watch two people. I began to watch a player by the name of Derrick Brooks, who is now a Hall of Fame linebacker. I began to watch how he moved and how he treated others. Everyone respected him, everyone listened to him when he spoke. As a player, I thought "man I want to be like that. I want to be respected on that level without doing all the negative stuff."

I also watched Coach Tony Dungy. He's a Super Bowl coach and the first African American head coach to win the Super Bowl. Every coach I had would be nice at first, but once they get you on the team, they tend to curse you out, say all types of stuff to you. I thought Coach Dungy would do the same thing. Well, one game we weren't playing well, and we went back to the locker room after having a bad first half and I thought he was going to curse us out. He talked the same way he did before we played badly. His character and integrity did not allow him to say curse words or call us out of our names.

He treated us like men, even when we weren't playing well. I thought to myself, "woah, this guy is different. This is not the same coach that I'm used to, and Derrick Brooks is not the same type of player I'm used to playing with." That taught me something—if these guys can do it, then I can do it. That's what motivated me to make character and integrity part of my platform. Dungy and Brooks were displaying it as part of their platform—and at a high level. Coach Dungy was one of the top coaches in the NFL before he retired. Derrick Brooks was one of the top linebackers who have ever played the game. To be able to see first-hand, an example of how-to walk-in character and integrity, and be in those type of positions, it motivated me, and I learned a lot by watching them.

Building a platform doesn't happen overnight, building your platform continues every day until the day you pass away. Do you have character? Do you tell the truth, work hard, persevere, study your craft, etc.? Have you found mentors to look up to like I did in this story. If not, look for someone positive to emulate right away. Finding a positive roll model or mentor will help you to build a strong platform and will be a crucial part of your success.

Define what platform means to you. For me a platform is a foundation that I invest my time and money in to help others in the future. You must put one block of faith down at a time. I have faith that if I move forward the next block will show up.

REFLECT

Think about it.

What is your definition of building a platform? *I am working on a lot of different projects and the time it takes to complete those projects can be tiresome sometimes. Why didn't I stop even when it got tough? Because I realized a platform can have several things going on at one time that you must learn to manage.*

TIME OUT WITH FRANK D. MUR-PHY: Remember what you do in the dark will always come to the light. Make sure what comes to the light is something that you want others to see and imitate.

What is your true purpose? *My true purpose is to speak to motivate others and create programs to build up the next generation. Identify your true purpose.*

Have you determined your values and are they in line with what you want your platform to be? *Identify your morals and values. Once you identify your morals and values, it will help you determine how you want to build your platform. Make sure your morals and values are positive. Do you have sex on the first date? Do you wear clothing that totally reveals your body? Do you use bad language all the time? If so, you may want to reevaluate your morals and values before building your platform.*

☐ **Yes**   ☐ **No**

TIME OUT WITH FRANK D. MURPHY: Remember if you get famous off of a lie, you will have to tell more lies to remain famous. Lies will always run out and truth will always outlast a lie.

Before you start your journey of legacy-building, determine what your passions are. These matched with your values will help you build a lasting legacy.

REFOCUS!

Refocus your Mind.

What contribution do you want to make to the world? *I created my legacy out of my pain and the mistakes that I overcame. So, I decided to help others that hurt like I used to hurt.*

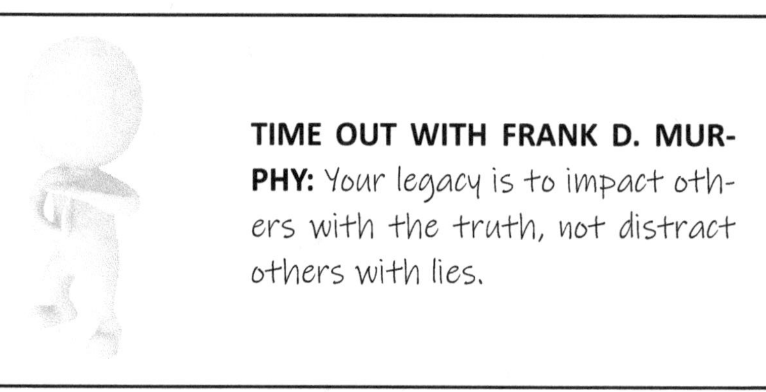

TIME OUT WITH FRANK D. MURPHY: Your legacy is to impact others with the truth, not distract others with lies.

Have you done your part in serving your community? *Do your part to make the world a better place. Don't worry about the fact that you can't do everything or that you can't do it perfectly.*

☐ **Yes**   ☐ **No**

Start creating and defining your platform. Make sure that your morals and values are consistent with your platform. If you have poor morals and values, no one will respond positively to your platform. You must have positive morals and values and allow your positive light to shine through for others to embrace your platform.

RESPOND!

Take action right **NOW!**

TIME OUT WITH FRANK D. MUR-PHY: What you don't do today, it is not guaranteed that you will get the opportunity to do it tomorrow. Get in motion RIGHT NOW.

PLAY 3 WRAP UP

Your platform can create opportunities for others to grow. Just look at the founder of Chick-fil-A. The restaurant is closed every Sunday, however their competitors are open on Sundays, yet Chick-fil-A is still the third highest grossing restaurant in the U.S. (behind McDonald's and Starbucks). Why do you think this is? Simple, it's because of the founder's platform. His platform was built on his beliefs, morals, and values, so he made it a priority for his employees to be off Sunday to attend church and spend time with family. In fact, Chick-fil-A's founder's platform stood so firmly on his belief in God that he taught children's bible study every Sunday for 30+ years. His company grew and he was instrumental in helping build the spiritual foundation of thousands of children over the years.

WHAT'S YOUR PLAN TO MASTER PLAY 3? Write it down!

HOW TO PUT DEFINITION BEHIND YOUR NAME

Play 4 is so important, especially if you want to be successful. Only you can put definition behind your name, people can help put definition behind your name, but nobody can define who you are but you. Others can assist with it, however you're actually the only one that determines your definition.

To understand putting definition behind your name, think of a dictionary. When you see a word, there's a definition behind it that tells you all about that word and that's what you remember every time you see or hear that word. That definition tells you or defines what that word means, what it stands for, and its description.

Well, when people see your name or they hear your name, what definition do they have behind it? What do people say when you walk out of the room? When you walk out of the room, what definition is behind your name.

Remember, you are the only one that can create your definition. If someone says you're lazy, okay, you put definition behind it and show that you're not lazy. What they say doesn't have to be the truth. The truth is going to be whatever you put out there for people to see behind your name.

FRANK'S STORY

One day my pastor and friend asked me to come sit in on a meeting. Now, there were billionaires and of course millionaires in this meeting. It was like a secret friendship with all of us meeting once a month to talk about different things going on in the local neighborhoods and in society. They discussed ideas of what we could do to make things better and things of that nature.

My pastor told me the reason why he wanted me to be a part of this meeting was because he knew I had experience with a lot of the issues, and I could provide some answers. So, I attended the first meeting, and I said nothing — I just listened. I came back next month for the second meeting, and I said nothing. At this point, the pastor was thinking, I know Frank knows what to say to help these guys out because this is what he does. I attended the third meeting, and again, I said nothing.

Finally, the pastor talked to me after the meeting. He said, "son why are you not saying anything? They need your advice. They need your help." I said, "I felt in my heart, that when you are around billionaires, you listen and you get to know every person in the room, so when you talk, you're talking to each individual in the room." I said, "you're not just talking to please one, you're talking to understanding each individual in that room. My heart didn't feel it should say anything until it is time"

So, when the next meeting came around, I spoke. I was able to speak to each and every one of them, because I got to know them before I spoke. I wasn't trying to prove to them that I knew all this stuff. Each of them had something they had a problem with. I made sure that I was able to speak to each of their situations, so I was able to break everything down from each standpoint that each of them had.

I tell people, when you're in the room with people of various levels you need to listen. That's not the time to try to prove that you should be in the room. It's not the time you're going to talk and try to show them that you have a good vocabulary. That's not the time to show them that you know what you're talking about. It's a time for you to humble yourself, sit back, and learn about each individual in that room, so when you do open your mouth, if the individuals ask you a question, you will know exactly what moves them because you took time out to get to know all of them on a level that most people don't.

Most people try to prove their worth, not walk in their worth. Stop trying to prove your worth and just walk in your worth and exercise your worth and everybody else will see the results.

TIME OUT WITH FRANK D. MURPHY: See only you can put definition behind your name. Others can help but only you put definition behind your name.

Do you often feel a strong desire to impress others or maintain a false image of what you want others to believe about you? If so, you are living a life of misplaced priorities. Your behavior is or will eventually leave you with little to no energy to carry out the important things in your life. It is normal to want others to see our successes, however, you shouldn't go over and beyond to impress others in order to get approval.

Break free from trying to impress others. Remember, you define who you are and there are going to be people who absolutely love who you are and there are going to be haters or people who are just not simply into you. No need to change who you are for anyone. You are perfect just the way you are.

REFLECT

Think about it.

What is the first impression others have of you? What definition do they put behind your name? *Do they define you as lazy, a troublemaker, a motivator, or hard worker?*

What do you need to change about yourself to allow others to view you how you would like to be viewed? *I put down my old playbook and picked up a new one so others would see me as a positive role model.*

Your desire to impress people is probably not always as effective as you think it is. Why? Because everyone sees success differently. Each of us has a different mission in life so success is going to be defined differently for every individual. For one person, success is giving up all material things and money to serve others in a 3rd world country. For someone else, it may be to make lots of money in the NBA. For another individual it may be to work two jobs to be the first in the family to attend college. From these three examples, success is defined and valued in totally different ways. This is exactly why some people are simply not going to be impressed by your desire to impress them with real or fake accomplishments. Spend time thinking about what success is to you and remember you don't need anyone to sign off on or approve of what you see as success.

REFOCUS!

Refocus your Mind.

Why do you think you need other people's approval to feel accomplished? *Are there people who if you don't have their approval or input you feel like you're a failure.*

It's time to accept that we can't control the opinions of others so you need to work on the things you can actually control. Spend time discovering who you really are and learn to love the person you are. Afterall, how are you going to love someone else if you don't love yourself? Every day you should remind yourself that there is no one as important as yourself.

RESPOND!

Take action right **NOW!**

PLAY 4 WRAP UP

Treat others how you would like to be treated. A simple, but powerful statement. If you master this art, it will reflect in how others view you. The impression others have of you (including first impression) will change drastically. Look at your definition this way – it's your personal brand or simply your identity.

WHAT IS YOUR PLAN TO MASTER PLAY 4? Write it down!

ACHIEVE GREATNESS WITH THE SECRET PLAY

First let's understand what greatness is. Greatness is when someone stands out from others, sets themselves apart and they work hard to be a leader in their field or craft.

Everybody knows greatness when they see it. Sometimes, when you see someone at the top of their field, or you listen to a successful person speak or you witness someone with mind-blowing talent, you feel a rush of inspiration. Are you the type of person that's motivated by that rush of inspiration or are you the type of person who looks on admiringly but assumes you don't have it in you to reach that level of greatness? If you assume greatness is unachievable, you are absolutely wrong. You just need the roadmap to greatness.

Here's the roadmap to achieving greatness:

- Create a vision. You must think about what you want in life. Without a vision, you won't know where to start.
- Turn adversity into your advantage. Take adversity in your life and use it as your fuel to take on challenges. Afterall, if you've overcome adversity in your life, why wouldn't you be able to overcome any other challenge in your life? We should learn and grow from our challenges. Adversity should make you stronger.
- Believe in yourself. Your past may make you feel like success and greatness is unachievable, but if you believe in yourself and your potential, you can do anything.
- Get your hustle on. Achieving greatness means you have to do what average people are unwilling to do. Hustle means sacrifice, sweat, hard work, long days, and determination. Read up on someone that is successful in your field. Did they sit back and wait for greatness, or did they get their hustle on to get it?
- Become the master of your mind, body, and soul. Be conscious of what you feed your mind, body, and soul. It's important to take care of yourself mentally and physically, and to build a spiritual foundation to ensure you are strong enough to pursue greatness. What do you put in your body? What negative things are you feeding your mind? Is your soul anchored in something greater than yourself?
- Serve others. What you set out to do should benefit not just yourself but others. Yes, you can achieve greatness and just focus on your own selfish agenda but think how fulfilling it would be to lift others up while achieving greatness. When you build giving back and serving others into your journey, I promise you that you'll find fulfillment and happiness along the way making your quest for greatness that much better.

Pursuing a life of greatness means a life of a constant hustle, learning and growing. Remember to serve others while on your journey. The happiness and fulfillment that you will feel while serving others makes achieving greatness all the more worth it.

FRANK'S STORY

I was eager to get back to playing football. I had waited and waited for a call from an NFL team, and I finally received that call. The General Manager (GM for short) offered me a contract. I was so excited that I immediately took the contract. However, during that point of my life, I was using my life skills curriculum program to mentor youth. When I took the contract, I did not think about the youth. Athletes don't typically turn down money because they love playing their sport.

I sat down and thought about those kids. I thought to myself, "man, I would be leaving them like everyone else has." So, I left great and reached for greatness when I decided to stay and mentor the youth. I called the GM back and told him that I couldn't take the contract because I had to finish what I had started. The GM couldn't believe it, but I knew if I wanted to go from great to greatness, I had to make a tough decision and finish what I started — I had to finish mentoring the kids.

As a football player, I worked relentlessly to become the type of player that I was. I had my share of ups and downs, but my continuous hard work allowed me to take care of my family while doing something that I loved to do. This is what it takes to become great.

I was a great football player, but I achieved greatness as a person by turning down the opportunity to play football to instead mentor children. Being great is to do what you love and help others out along the way. Achieving greatness is to fulfill your God-given purpose and to help those around you, including the one's outside of your family, who need it most.

Getting out of your comfort zone is getting out of the box that other people have put you in, and the limitations that others have put on you to be successful. What steps will you take to get out of your comfort zone? The dictionary says the comfort zone is a place where "you feel comfortable and your abilities are not being tested," and is a place where "you don't have to do anything new or different." In other words, your comfort zone is a place where you are stagnant, and you don't make much of an effort to do anything different.

To achieve greatness, you must be able to embrace new experiences. Embracing new experiences can change your life and the direction of your career, your talent, your relationships, etc. Make sure the new experiences that you have are calculated risks. Think about the consequences of you making these decisions and how it will affect your life and impact your success. There are *no shortcuts* to being successful with your new playbook. If you take any shortcuts to success, then you will not get the results you are expecting.

If I stayed in my comfort zone, I would have taken the contract the GM offered me so that I could return to the NFL. But because I was willing to step out of my comfort zone to achieve greatness, I made the decision to mentor the youth, which was one of the best decisions I have ever made.

In order to achieve greatness, you must stay focused on improving yourself each and every day, even if you feel like your life is in a good place at the moment. You must also be willing to step out of your comfort zone. Have you made any effort to step out of your comfort zone? If not, take some time to think about stepping out of your comfort zone and how it will affect your going from great to greatness.

Think about it.

What is holding you back from achieving greatness? *Is it because you believe that your life is already great? Or are you okay with how your life is going at the moment?*

Are you focused on improving every day to achieve greatness?

☐ **Yes**   ☐ **No**

TIME OUT WITH FRANK D. MUR-PHY: Create a to-do list every day. Once you finish something on your to-do list, check it off and move on to the next task. Keeping a to-do list will stop you from being stagnant and help you stay focused on improving each day.

Are you humble and willing enough to consider other people's knowledge or wisdom to help you reach greatness?

☐ **Yes**   ☐ **No**

Do you have a mentor? *In order to reach greatness, you should consider other people's wisdom. In other words, on the road to greatness, it is beneficial to have a mentor who shows you the ropes.*

☐ **Yes**   ☐ **No**

TIME OUT WITH FRANK D. MUR-PHY: In order to reach the level of success you want to reach; you must surround yourself with people who have achieved what you're trying to achieve. Create a list of potential mentors. A mentor is a successful person that you can shadow and reach out to ask for direction.

Are you willing to take direction from someone else who wants to help you see another perspective?

☐ **Yes**   ☐ **No**

Will you be open to correction? *Having a mentor, their maybe times when you will be corrected if you are doing something wrong.*

☐ **Yes**   ☐ **No**

Are you willing to switch up your routine in order to step out of your comfort zone and reach greatness? We refer to our comfort zone as a comfort zone because it is where we feel safe and comfortable. When we step out of our comfort zone, we typically feel some level of anxiety. Because of this, some people make it a point to never step out of their comfort zone. The only problem is that if you don't take the steps to step out of your comfort zone, you may never reach the level of greatness you are meant to reach.

Stepping out of your comfort zone can start with making changes in your daily routine, your diet, your habits, your surroundings, etc. Simple changes will set you on a path to achieve small victories that lead to bigger victories.

REFOCUS!

Refocus your Mind.

In what ways are you willing to switch up your routine to reach greatness? *Are you willing to wake up 30 minutes early, work late into the evening, work on weekends?*

FRANK'S CHALLENGE

Take a blank sheet of paper and write down all the things that you do in your routine. Consider these things what you do in your comfort zone. Now write down a few new things that you can include in your routine. Just by doing this, you have expanded your routine to include things that are outside of your comfort zone.

Are you willing to cut off the people in your life who are holding you back from reaching greatness? *It is possible that you are not where you want to be because there are people in your life who are weighing you down or dimming your light. It may be necessary to eliminate unnecessary people who God may not have intended to be in your life by the time you reach greatness.*

□ **Yes**   □ **No**

Get comfortable with discomfort. If you don't experience discomfort, it's because you are doing the same thing and have become numb to doing something different to help you reach greatness.

Take baby steps to get started. Once you start venturing out of your comfort zone, you will make bigger and longer steps.

RESPOND!

Take action right **NOW!**

Are you willing to start taking baby steps to achieve greatness? *If you answered yes, write down some ways you will start taking baby steps.*

☐ **Yes**   ☐ **No**

Ask yourself, have you done all you can do to seek greatness?

☐ **Yes**   ☐ **No**

PLAY 5 WRAP UP

In order to leave great to seek out greatness, you must sacrifice three things—you must sacrifice your selfishness, you must sacrifice your last success story, and you have to sacrifice your last failure. Are you willing to make these sacrifices?

☐ **Yes**   ☐ **No**

WHAT'S YOUR PLAN TO MASTER PLAY 5? Write it down!

STOP CARRYING THE RIGHT PLAYBOOK BUT WITH THE WRONG TEAM

The team that you are carrying your playbook with is the circle that you hang around, and the circle that you are hanging around is most likely running the same plays. You need to understand that your team is not someone who agrees with everything you say, your team is not someone who caters to your weaknesses or insecurities. Your team shouldn't tell you that you missed your opportunity. Your team should always be willing to correct you when there is need for correction. If this isn't happening, it may be time for you to reevaluate your team.

You can't bring the same playbook to different teams. You're with a new team now, so create a new playbook. I had to realize I was carrying the wrong playbook with a different team. When you go around different circles, you have to know what playbook you're carrying so that you can fit in. You have to do your due diligence on who you are hanging around.

FRANK'S STORY

I remember the moment I realized I was carrying the wrong playbook while trying to be successful in the NFL. I was still hanging around the wrong people although I knew it was time for me to put down the old playbook. I was in the NFL, yet I was still hanging around friends from my old neighborhood. I went back to my old neighborhood like I usually did to hang out with them and show them love and I had a friend who pulled out a gun and started shooting at a man across the street from us.

He didn't care that his actions could affect my career. He started to have a shootout right in front of me. We ran and I got to the porch of his house, and everybody was in the house but me. I was on the porch thinking, "what am I doing?" and "why am I around here?" As soon as I started asking myself those questions a car pulled up, a guy pulled out a chopper (gun) and was prepared to shoot up the entire house and I was the only one on the porch.

When he recognized it was me, he said "Frank, man you better talk to your people. I respect you, but you have to talk to your people." He was about to kill me on the spot because he was going to shoot the whole house up but because I was standing on the porch, I saved everyone in the house. If I was in the house, the entire house would have been shot up and everyone would have been dead. I realized that I wanted to carry the right playbook but with the wrong team. I was blessed to be in the NFL, but I am still trying to live around the street life.

You have to surround yourself with the right team. When you are on a mission to reach your goal, having the right team in your life can help you reach your target more effectively. The wrong team brings wrong thinking, wrong thinking brings wrong decisions, wrong decisions bring wrong results. Evaluate your team so that you won't do the wrong things. When was the last time you evaluated your team? Sometimes, not even your best friend is part of your team for advancing in life, relationships, or business. Sometimes your best friend is just as blind as you are because you think the same way. Don't always depend on your best friend to be the one that helps you advance.

Everybody has a roll to play. Your best friend may not be the one who helps you get to the next level. When I was on that porch, fearing for my life, it was then that I realized that I was not surrounded by the right team. I was around a team that only thought about themselves first. Not the advancement of my life.

You must have enough courage to remove the negative people from your life. Letting go of the relationships that aren't benefiting you is a critical step if you want to become more positive and successful. If you don't get rid of the dead weight, you won't make it to the team that is meant to help you be successful.

The new team that you need will always be moving forward fast, but your dead weight will not allow you to catch up to your new team because you "respectfully" feel committed to dead weight friends. Removing negative people from your life will also allow you to become the person you truly want to be. Negative people will always give you negativity if you keep allowing them to give it to you.

Removing negative people from your life will free yourself from constant judgment, negativity, and lack of support. If you want to make a positive change in your life, remember, the people around you have a significant influence on your energy, growth, and potential for success.

TIME OUT WITH FRANK D. MURPHY: Don't bring your millionaire mentality to a billionaire circle. You must study and do your due diligence on the team that you will be around.

Take an honest look at the team you surround yourself with right now. Are you surrounded by the right team? Are your current team members positive or negative additions to your team?

Once you've evaluated your team, think about the ways you need to go about removing the negative people from your team.

REFLECT

Think about it.

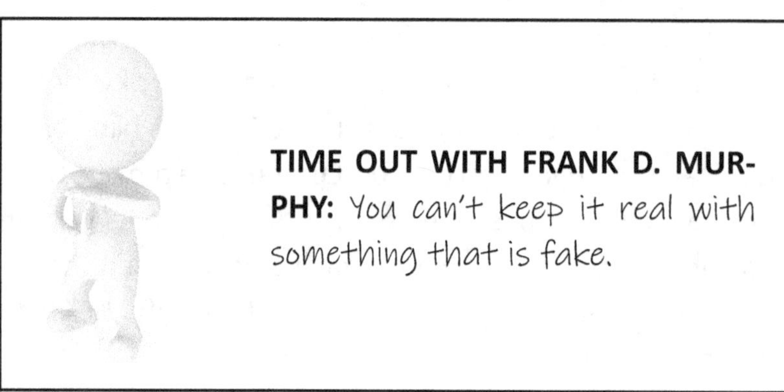

TIME OUT WITH FRANK D. MURPHY: *You can't keep it real with something that is fake.*

Is your current team an average team or a great team?

Think about where you want to go in life. Is this the team that you want heading into the future? *Does your circle support you; do they push you, and do they correct you if you are wrong?*

☐ **Yes** ☐ **No**

Think about each part your circle needs to play in your life for you to be successful. Ask yourself if your friends fit any of those parts?

☐ **Yes** ☐ **No**

FRANK'S CHALLENGE

Take a blank sheet of paper and write down all the positive attributes that you need from your friends. Then write down the friends that meet all those attributes (supportive, critical when they need to be, on their grind as well, etc.). If they don't, slowly distance yourself from these friends, and find a better circle of friends that are more of a fit for the success you plan to have in life.

Reduce your interactions with friends, coworkers and family members who are negative, discouraging, and bitter. This is one of the most important things you can do for yourself in order to find success in creating your new team.

Stay away from people who find fault in every single thing you do. They will be more focused on tearing you down than building you up.

REFOCUS!

Refocus your Mind.

What steps will you take to stop interacting with the people who are not helping you reach your potential? *Example: not participating in meaningless conversations that compete with your positive thinking.*

Are you participating in meaningless conversations? *For example, are you on the phone all day participating in meaningless gossip?*

☐ Yes   ☐ No

Do you have friends like this?

☐ Yes   ☐ No

Begin your quest to surround yourself with positive and successful people. Find new, like-minded friends, or find a positive coach or mentor. Share your ideas only with people who have the vision to see what you are trying to accomplish.

RESPOND!

Take action right
NOW!

Does your circle support you; do they push you; do they correct you if you are wrong?

☐ Yes   ☐ No

You can only do what you have knowledge in. Do you have a mentor?

☐ Yes   ☐ No

PLAY 6 WRAP UP

While you don't get to choose who your relatives are, you can – and should – choose who gets to be on your team. Make sure you choose wisely.

WHAT'S YOUR PLAN TO MASTER PLAY 6? Write it down!

IS ANGER OR ANGUISH PART OF YOUR SECRET PLAYBOOK?

Put down your old playbook of anger and pick up your new book of anguish. You must know the difference between anger and anguish to be successful. Anguish is a burning desire on the inside of you to assist or help someone who you see being misused, mistreated, or hurt. That burning desire on the inside of you will push you in a direction to impact someone's life. Anger is a strong feeling of being annoyed, displeased, or bitter. How do you walk—in anger or anguish?

If your answer is anguish, you're headed in the right direction, but if you answered anger, you're headed in the wrong direction. Now you know why it's been hard for you to be successful in life. Anger will take you further than you will ever want to go down the wrong path and have you doing things you never want to do. If you walk in anger and try to fulfill your purpose and be successful in life, it will not happen because your anger emotion will cause you to make bad decisions along the way.

FRANK'S STORY

When I was in the NFL, I remember doing a toy give-away one year for Christmas. I was so excited to do this toy give-away because I always give away a bunch of toys to the youth. This year I ran out of toys because there were so many kids. I felt so bad for the children, so I drove to Walmart and bought a bunch of toys, loaded up my truck and drove back. When I returned, the children and their parents had already left so I asked around for their address.

They lived in a neighborhood that I did not need to be in because of my past when I was in the streets. I was not cool with the people in that particular neighborhood. I ended up still going into those apartments in my brand-new truck and I found the family. I risked my life to deliver those toys to those children. I had a burning desire on the inside of me to see those children smile because I knew they were so hurt that we ran out of toys. When I found them, I went up to their home. Their living conditions were not ideal, but I still went in to make them feel comfortable and I brought them all the toys.

That's anguish! A burning desire to help someone in need. I would never advise someone to go into a situation that could harm them, but I felt that is what I had to do at that particular time.

TIME OUT WITH FRANK D. MUR-PHY: Anger will take you further than you will ever want to go. Anger will make you stay longer than you wanted to stay. So, make sure you have your anger in check.

At this point of your journey, are you operating in anger or anguish? Think about how you deal with different situations and make sure you know the difference.

Think about it.

Has there been times in your life when you let anger drive your decision-making?

☐ Yes   ☐ No

Do you understand what angers you?

☐ Yes   ☐ No

How long has anger been a driving force in your life? *Anguish will push you to think about more than yourself. Anger will push you to think about only you. This is why you've made a lot of bad decisions and have not arrived at your successful place.*

To not operate in anger, you need to know and understand the warning signs of anger. If you know the warning signs or what triggers anger in you, perhaps you would avoid certain situations. Here's a few warning signs and triggers of anger: knots in your stomach, clenching your hands or jaw, feeling clammy or flushed, breathing faster, headaches, pacing or needing to walk around, seeing "red", and having trouble concentrating. If you experience any of these signs or triggers, make every effort to avoid situations that anger you and think before responding.

Refocus your Mind.

IS ANGER OR ANGUISH PART OF YOUR SECRET PLAYBOOK?

Put down your old playbook of anger and pick up your new book of anguish. You must know the difference between anger and anguish to be successful. Anguish is a burning desire on the inside of you to assist or help someone who you see being misused, mistreated, or hurt. That burning desire on the inside of you will push you in a direction to impact someone's life. Anger is a strong feeling of being annoyed, displeased, or bitter. How do you walk—in anger or anguish?

If your answer is anguish, you're headed in the right direction, but if you answered anger, you're headed in the wrong direction. Now you know why it's been hard for you to be successful in life. Anger will take you further than you will ever want to go down the wrong path and have you doing things you never want to do. If you walk in anger and try to fulfill your purpose and be successful in life, it will not happen because your anger emotion will cause you to make bad decisions along the way.

FRANK'S STORY

When I was in the NFL, I remember doing a toy give-away one year for Christmas. I was so excited to do this toy give-away because I always give away a bunch of toys to the youth. This year I ran out of toys because there were so many kids. I felt so bad for the children, so I drove to Walmart and bought a bunch of toys, loaded up my truck and drove back. When I returned, the children and their parents had already left so I asked around for their address.

They lived in a neighborhood that I did not need to be in because of my past when I was in the streets. I was not cool with the people in that particular neighborhood. I ended up still going into those apartments in my brand-new truck and I found the family. I risked my life to deliver those toys to those children. I had a burning desire on the inside of me to see those children smile because I knew they were so hurt that we ran out of toys. When I found them, I went up to their home. Their living conditions were not ideal, but I still went in to make them feel comfortable and I brought them all the toys.

That's anguish! A burning desire to help someone in need. I would never advise someone to go into a situation that could harm them, but I felt that is what I had to do at that particular time.

TIME OUT WITH FRANK D. MURPHY: Anger will take you further than you will ever want to go. Anger will make you stay longer than you wanted to stay. So, make sure you have your anger in check.

At this point of your journey, are you operating in anger or anguish? Think about how you deal with different situations and make sure you know the difference.

REFLECT

Think about it.

Has there been times in your life when you let anger drive your decision-making?

☐ Yes   ☐ No

Do you understand what angers you?

☐ Yes   ☐ No

How long has anger been a driving force in your life? *Anguish will push you to think about more than yourself. Anger will push you to think about only you. This is why you've made a lot of bad decisions and have not arrived at your successful place.*

To not operate in anger, you need to know and understand the warning signs of anger. If you know the warning signs or what triggers anger in you, perhaps you would avoid certain situations. Here's a few warning signs and triggers of anger: knots in your stomach, clenching your hands or jaw, feeling clammy or flushed, breathing faster, headaches, pacing or needing to walk around, seeing "red", and having trouble concentrating. If you experience any of these signs or triggers, make every effort to avoid situations that anger you and think before responding.

REFOCUS!

Refocus your Mind.

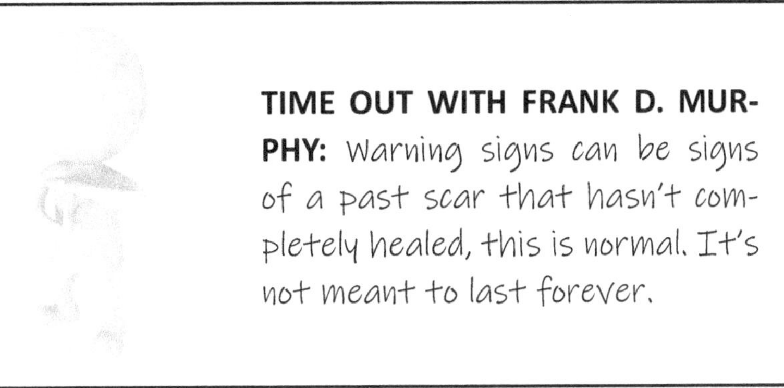

TIME OUT WITH FRANK D. MUR-PHY: Warning signs can be signs of a past scar that hasn't completely healed, this is normal. It's not meant to last forever.

What are your warning signs? *If someone did something to anger me, I would breathe hard. That was my warning sign to let me know that I was starting to get angry. Think before you speak.*

Do you think before you speak? *When you speak it brings life or death to the atmosphere. Think about the consequences three times before you speak. What are you bringing into the atmosphere? What are you speaking into your atmosphere?*

☐ **Yes**   ☐ **No**

FRANK'S CHALLENGE

Use 15 minutes a day to meditate and speak positive things over and over to yourself. Get rid of what is causing you to anger.

Are you ready to take the steps to get rid of what is causing you anger?

☐ **Yes**   ☐ **No**

From this point forward, let anguish drive you. Identify your burning desires and use that to drive your decision-making. Sometimes we respond to situations in anger because of fear. Talk to someone about your fears that you trust. You must have accountability. When you are in a moment of anger, think about the consequences of your actions 3 times. Say it to yourself under your breath. If I act on it, I'll go to jail, loose my family, or even get killed. If you don't have someone you feel comfortable talking to consider visiting *www.opencounseling.com*. They will help you find someone to talk to.

Take action right **NOW!**

PLAY 7 WRAP UP

Identify your fears. If you are angry, that means that you fear something. Write down what you fear when it comes to your anger.

Identify your triggers. There are constant situations in your life that may trigger you. If you know your triggers, when a situation arrives that triggers anger, you will know how to respond.

WHAT'S YOUR PLAN TO MASTER PLAY 7? Write it down!

TRADE IN YOUR FANTASIES FOR THE SECRET PLAY

Stop letting people live fantasies through you and stop living fantasies through other people. We live in a society where people have fallen "in love" with celebrities, movie stars, supermodels, athletes, entertainers, rappers, Instagram models, etc., but the problem is that they are falling in love with the "idea" of these individuals, and not the "real" person.

In relationships, how can you tell if that man or woman is living a fantasy through, you? If that man or woman is not giving you all of them, but they want everything from you, that means that they are attempting to have a fantasy lived through you, for you to replace something that they can't give. A person that lives a fantasy through you will ask things of you that they will not provide and do for others or themselves.

In business there is no way that you can have a business partner and you are only giving 30% and they are giving 70%. In business relationships, your partner expects you to be qualified based on what you told them you were qualified to do. They were expecting more out of you but when they got a chance to know you, they realized you weren't qualified. They were expecting more out of you, but they can't get that out of you, because you were living a fantasy that you could do those things. You were shooting them a dream and telling them a fantasy, but then they came and exposed you because when they connected with you in business, they found out that you couldn't do those things. You must make sure that you are not living a fantasy and that someone is not living a fantasy through you.

The main thing you should look for in a relationship or business partner is consistency. Without the word consistency, you have someone who is just running games and playing games. They are making you a part of their games until you wake up and realize that you were just part of the game.

Do not allow someone to fall in love with the idea of you, and do not allow yourself to fall in love with the idea of others. When fantasy becomes our reality, we may find we've fallen in love with a dream, fallen in love with an idea, but ultimately, fallen in love with a lie.

FRANK'S STORY

During a game when I was playing for the Tampa Bay Buccaneers, I was standing back getting ready to receive the kickoff. While I was waiting for the ball to be kicked, I noticed just how loud the stadium was from all the fans' cheers. It was in that moment that I realized if I was to get hurt, or someone else was to take my position, it would be another player replacing me, and the fans would be just as loud, clapping and cheering for them the same way. I realized that at the end of the day, it wasn't about who was on the field, it was about the fans living a fantasy through whoever was on the field.

I want you to understand to not let anyone live a fantasy through you. Fan is short for fantasy. Other people will live a fantasy through you based on entertainment. Don't let anyone live a fantasy through you because it will never be enough. You will end up getting caught up in a constant attempt to please something or someone that will never be pleased.

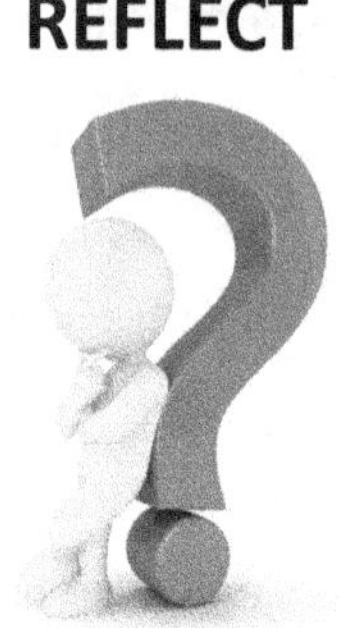

REFLECT

Think about your relationships. How many of your relationships are fantasies? You may act a certain way around certain people to make them happy when you're not happy yourself. Are you always genuine with others? Take time to reflect on your relationships with friends, family, coworkers, neighbors, classmates, or significant others. Evaluate whether you are living in a fantasy with the important individuals in your life.

Think about it.

Have there ever been a time in your life when you were so obsessed with someone that you had to have it or wanted to be them? *If you checked yes, you have been living a fantasy.*

☐ **Yes**   ☐ **No**

What are a few ways that you can focus your attention on improving your life rather than focusing on someone else's life?

Who or what are you focused on? *If you are focusing your attention mostly on others and not yourself, you are focusing on the wrong things.*

Identify the people or things that are causing you to fantasize. Identifying the root of your fantasies can help you determine why you have them.

Reshape your mind. To stop creating fantasies in your mind of other things or people, you must reshape your mind to think of ways to improve yourself.

Refocus your Mind.

Do you know the root of your fantasies?

☐ **Yes**   ☐ **No**

Focus on reality!

No more procrastinating, daydreaming, and fantasizing. It's time to focus on your reality.

Take action right **NOW!**

PLAY 8 WRAP UP

Since fantasizing can be an escape mechanism, you should learn to deal with your fantasies directly. Work on redirecting your thoughts and increasing your concentration so that you can become more focused on yourself. Make simple changes in your life to begin living the life that was meant for you (not others). Instead of watching others live out their dreams, start pursuing your dreams. Stop spending so much time on social media wishing you had what others have. Stop seeking out celebrity gossip. Stop binge watching reality TV. Start taking the steps you need to take to make your dreams a reality.

WHAT'S MY PLAN TO MASTER PLAY 8? Write it down!

BRINGING YOUR OLD PLAYBOOK INTO THE PRESENT COULD ALTER YOUR FUTURE

A lot of times we hold on to our old playbook because the old playbook is familiar, so you become comfortable. You're going to have to break that familiarity. It's hard breaking old habits to get into new habits, but one thing that we're trying to teach you is that the new habit is going to take you to a whole new level. It's going to break you free from toxic behaviors, drama and all the trauma that you've been experiencing.

I just really want you to understand that you're going to have to get rid of some of your old ways, your old thinking, your old habits, and you're going to have to step out on faith and switch completely over to the new playbook. If you don't, you will not be successful, and you'll be going in one big circle for the rest of your life. This applies to business, relationships, marriage, and all phases of life.

A self-audit will help you to make sure that you aren't allowing plays from the old playbook to sneak back into your life.

FRANK'S STORY

When I played for the Tampa Bay Buccaneers, I studied the plays, went out on the field, and performed at a high level. But when I left to go to the Miami Dolphins, because I got offered more money or the opportunity was different, I couldn't take the Tampa Bay Buccaneers playbook with me and think that I would be successful. Miami is a whole other organization. They have a whole new system. They have a whole different playbook.

No matter how good I was, how fast I was, how quick I was or how explosive I was. In fact, I had the record for the 40 — I ran a 42.1. None of that matters if I don't have the right playbook to run the correct plays for the new team. When I went to Miami, I had to learn a new playbook all over again to be successful. It didn't matter how hard it was, no matter what, if I wanted to be successful and make that team and be on the Miami Dolphins team and make the money that I was looking to make, I would have to relearn a different playbook. I couldn't bring Tampa Bay's plays and the same mindset over to Miami.

So, in life, what I'm trying to get you to understand, you're going to have to switch that old playbook for your new playbook to reach the level of success you desire.

Think of a time in your life when you were faced with adversity. How did you handle it? Was there a time when you realized you had to let go of your old way of doing things (plays from your old playbook) to do things a new way (plays from your new playbook)?

Think about it.

FRANK'S CHALLENGE

Anger will take you further than you will ever want to go. Anger will make you stay longer than you wanted to stay. So, I challenge you to make sure you have your anger in check.

Review both your old playbook AND your new playbook. Do you find any similarities in both playbooks?

☐ **Yes** ☐ **No**

Why do you think your old playbook is so different from your new playbook?

Allow yourself to be open. Open to suggestions, open to new ideas, and open to change. When you are open to change, eliminating your old ways to develop new ways will become much easier to accomplish.

Refocus your Mind.

Are you open to suggestions or new ideas?

☐ **Yes**   ☐ **No**

If you answered no, why do you think you are not open to suggestions and new ideas?

Moving on from the past isn't easy but it certainly is possible. You must remember that your past mistakes are not permanent. You can move on from them.

When you find yourself creeping back into old behaviors, consider using the Mirror Drill. This exercise is simple. Look in the mirror and repeat one or all of the following affirmations to yourself:

- I will not allow my past to affect my future.
- I will see results.
- I am successful.
- I will leave a lasting legacy.
- I will overcome every obstacle in my way.
- I will prosper financially.
- I am ready for change.
- I will not fold under pressure
- I am handsome/beautiful.
- Nothing can stop me.

You can speak positive things into existence. That doesn't mean that you won't still have bad things happen in your life, but you will start looking at those bad things as new obstacles to overcome.

RESPOND!

Take action right
NOW!

PLAY 9 WRAP UP

Work hard every day to get rid of your old playbook and accept the new one. Once you do, you will start to see new developments in your life. Don't fight the newness in your life. We fight and try to control what we don't know or understand. People tend to fight off the newness because the oldness is so familiar. Just because you don't know what's going to happen don't fear it.

Next time you are in a difficult situation, pay attention to how you respond. If you respond similarly to past situations, you may have used your old playbook instead of your new one. Remember to clean your residue (remove your old playbook) so that when difficult situations occur, you will remember to respond with your new playbook (in a new and improved way).

WHAT'S MY PLAN TO MASTER PLAY 9? Write it down!

TIME TO LET GO OF THE OWNER OF THE OLD PLAYBOOK

You keep going back to the owner of the old playbook where the pain was created and asking them to help you get rid of the pain. Or you're thinking the owner of the old playbook is going to change to help get rid of the pain that they created. That's what I see a lot of people doing in relationships.

How are you going to go back to the one that caused you pain and think they're going to change in order to make things better for you. It's nothing that they can do. It's now up to you to make better decisions and you're going to have to let them go.

You can't depend on somebody else to make you happy, you have got to depend on yourself to make changes to make you happy because the owner(s) of your old playbook have proven to you time and time again that this is their system. This is who they are, and they have consistently shown you who they are. They created the playbook they presented to you, and that playbook should no longer be a part of your life if you're trying to go to a new level. If you're trying to go to a new level in business as an entrepreneur, or new levels in relationships, you can't keep the same playbook and you can't go back to the person who created the old playbook and ask them to help you change.

So often, I find this happening. For example, a person hurt someone by cheating them out of millions of dollars. The person went back to them to try to get the thief to make it right. The thief had already shown their character and burned the person, so why would they ask the thief to change how they do things for them. They had known them for 10, 15, 20 years and that's who they have always been. And that's the same thing in relationships, we want somebody to change, it's not about them changing its about you changing and making the adjustments to get away from the drama, that trauma, and that toxicness.

FRANK'S CHALLENGE

I'm challenging you to stop begging the owner of your hurt/ mess to change for you or to help you change. The owner that created your mess, created your trauma and your toxicness. It's time to step out of the shadow of the owner of the old playbook.

FRANK'S STORY

When I played for the Chicago Bears, every night I would hang out with some of the players and party until 5 a.m. the next morning, knowing I had practice in the morning. So, when I went to Tampa Bay, I kept that same playbook, same attitude, and same habits. I kept the same old playbook but was expecting different results. I had to realize that I can't beg the friends that led me to do the things I was doing, to change so I can change. I had to get to Tampa and say, "you know what, I got to create a whole different playbook for who I want to be now." I couldn't beg them to change, I had to make the adjustments for myself.

I couldn't tell my friends (owners of the old playbook), to put the play book down and stop what they were doing, I had to decide for myself that I wanted a new movement (new playbook). I had to find out what players on this new team were trying to do something different, something new. And that's what I did.

That's how I learned how to start doing more productive stuff. I started helping out in the community, going to do speaking engagements, doing toy drives, etc. I was no longer 100% focused on going out.

So, you can't ask the owners of your old playbook to change. You have to make the change for yourself.

Review your playbook (the way in which you live your life). Are you the owner of your current playbook or is someone else? Determine whether your current playbook is the playbook you really want for your future. Think about the things you can do to improve your playbook.

REFLECT

Think about it.

Has your current playbook been successful? Do you need a new playbook?

In what ways can you change your playbook in order for your life to change for the better?

The first step of letting go of the owner of your old playbook is to acknowledge the truth about the toxic person or people and to stop justifying and rationalizing their behaviors. You must realize that you can't change their behaviors and that they are not going to change to make you happy. I realize you have history with a lot of these individuals, but you must remember that there is a season for everything and everyone. Sometimes those individuals are just not meant to be in your new season.

Refocus your Mind.

Do you think it's possible to move on from the individual(s) from your old playbook?

☐ **Yes**   ☐ **No**

Are you finding it hard to move on because you have history with the individual? *You grew up with them; they were your first love; or it's one of your relatives.*

☐ **Yes**   ☐ **No**

Now that you've made the decision to let go of the owner of your old playbook, you must now decide how to end the relationship. I suggest you either quit cold turkey or wean yourself off the person(s) and just let the relationship fade away. If you choose to wean yourself off, slowly decrease your communication and time spent with the person.

Once you've ended the relationship, remember to forgive the person. Remember you played a part in the relationship so you can't totally blame them for all your drama and trauma. Besides, forgiving them is good for your own healing. You also want to give yourself time to grieve the loss of the relationship. It is natural to feel sad.

Take action right **NOW!**

PLAY 10 WRAP UP

You must hold yourself accountable for the decisions you made and not blame the one who introduced the playbook to you. Once you've held yourself accountable, change how you choose and make choices. You should no longer involve yourself with someone who is a stripper, drug dealer, lazy, or someone who is not motivated. These people simply don't have a place in your new playbook.

WHAT'S MY PLAN TO MASTER PLAY 10? Write it down!

DO YOU SEE THINGS AS AN OPPORTUNITY OR AN OBLIGATION?

How do you see things in your life? Are you treating situations like an opportunity or an obligation? Let's make sure you understand the difference between the two. Obligation means you treat situations like you're just going through the motions. If you treat situations as an opportunity, you're looking at the situation as a blessing in disguise. You take full advantage of an opportunity. If you look at it as an obligation, you're not going to take full advantage of it. Cease the moment every chance you get. Whether it's with a job, with your parents, or a relationship, it may be an opportunity that you may not ever get again.

Is your reaction in times of adversity good or bad? It's only going to be how you see it. You can find negative in every single thing that happens to you — that's not hard to do. I mean everything in life you can find negative in, but you can also find positive in everything that happens in your life. It's just that we don't look for the positive in situations because we've been trained to look for negatives in everything.

So, what I'm trying to say, can we retrain you to see things differently? Can we retrain you in play 11, because you can look at things as an opportunity or an obligation.

FRANK'S STORY

When I played for Miami, I was tearing it up. I was the last receiver that they picked up as a free agent. I signed my contract and got started. They already had eight receivers, I came in and within a week, I moved from the ninth receiver to the fifth receiver. So, I'm on my way up. By the next week, I was like the third or fourth receiver. Just that quick in two weeks. So, I'm thinking I have a great chance at a spot on the team. I'm doing good.

Nick Saban was the head coach of the Miami Dolphins at that time. He is now the Alabama head coach and the best coach to ever do it in college football. That was his first year trying out the NFL, and he didn't understand it's not college, it's the NFL.

It came time to release some of the players and he released me, and I was one of the top five receivers on the team. The receiver coach brought me in the office, and I told him that Coach Saban had just released me. He couldn't believe that the Coach released me without talking to him first. — besides, I was in the top receiver rotation. So, he went into Coach Saban's office and started arguing with him. They're going back and forth and then the receiver coach comes out of the office all red. He said he didn't think it was right and that he would have never released me because there were many other receivers that they could release considering I was already in the rotation.

I thought to myself, how should I see this moment? How should I see this adversity. I'm getting released and I have a great contract (about a million dollars). When it was all said and done, I went back to Nick Saban and said, "I want to thank you for this opportunity. I appreciate you Coach Saban. I appreciate you for bringing me in". I then left. I didn't get all mad like most players and curse him out. I handled it how I saw it – as an opportunity.

So, I got in my car and I'm riding back to Tampa, Florida, and suddenly I felt something in my heart urging me to go to Jacksonville. So, I called my pastor and told him that I was heading back to Tampa, but I had this feeling that I needed to go to Jacksonville. He told me that I needed to follow my heart. And that's exactly what I did.

As soon as I got across the Jacksonville line, my phone rang, and it was my mom letting me know that my dad was dying. So I went straight to the hospital, I parked my car in front of the hospital and ran to my father's room. I left my brand-new Mercedes Benz running with all my brand-new designer clothes and shoes. I didn't even lock the door. I got out of the car, shut the door, and started running with the car on.

As I ran into the room where my dad and my family were, they were shocked I was there. I told them it was a long story and asked that everyone, but my mom, leave the room. My brothers, sisters, and other relatives and friends left.

My dad was suffering from diabetes, Alzheimer's, and other ailments. I asked him if he wanted to live, and he said yes. So, I prayed over him, and my dad lived three, four more years even though they said he was going to die that day.

It turns out my unfortunate release from Miami turned into an awesome opportunity.

So, it's how you see things. You can't always look at things as negative. Just because something bad happens doesn't mean there's going to be a bad ending. You can't write your own book. You can't end your book right there on a bad note. You have to make sure you're creating a positive atmosphere. Positive thinking will help you to be successful.

How do you see things? How are you looking at things? I challenge you that when adversity hits, immediately think of the positive. What positive can come out of this? Now, it's not going to be easy, but I'm asking you to fight through negative emotions, bad habits, and to fight through what you usually do when something bad happens. If you can fight through, trust me, you will find something positive. It may not be that same day, but if you keep searching, you will find not only one or two positive things, but you will also start to see four or five or maybe six positive reasons of why something happened.

REFLECT

Think about it.

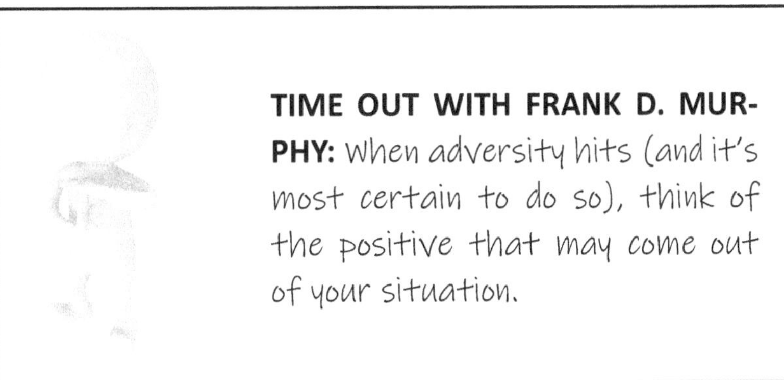

Write down 3 situations in your life that you saw as an obligation but that turned out to be an opportunity. *Include how you are or did benefit from the opportunity today.*

Sometimes our day-to-day obligations can overwhelm us. When that happens, we start to get burned out and sometimes we start neglecting our obligations. Change your mindset and look at every situation (good and bad) as an opportunity. Once you do your whole outlook will change.

Begin to see every obligation or situation as an opportunity and respond as if there may be a new opportunity on the horizon with every situation. Each opportunity could possibly be an opportunity to serve, earn, learn, influence, network, encourage, teach, etc.

REFOCUS!

Refocus your Mind.

FRANK'S CHALLENGE

I challenge you to look at every obligation or situation from this moment forward as an opportunity. I promise you it will change your life.

Write down 5 of your day-to-day obligations like school, work, caring for siblings/children, etc. Now next to each one, write down what opportunity you can take advantage of through each obligation. *You learn new things in school which increase your chances of a good future. You learn to be a good parent caring for your siblings, or you receive undying love for caring for your own kids. You make money to take care of yourself when you work.*

If you look at people who have endured a tremendous amount of heartache or at people who are great at what they do, if you listen to their interviews or read up on them, the common thread is they focused on the opportunity before them. They didn't dwell on how tired they were, or how hard it was. I'm not saying they didn't get tired, or they didn't go through trials, it just was not what they focused on. They focused solely on the opportunity they were blessed with.

RESPOND!

Take action right **NOW!**

PLAY 11 WRAP UP

Examine how often you complain about your responsibilities. Do you complain often? If so, you may view your responsibilities as an obligation. Instead of complaining, try treating your responsibilities as areas to be grateful for. If you become grateful for every responsibility you have, then you will have a better chance of treating these responsibilities as opportunities to be better.

WHAT'S MY PLAN TO MASTER PLAY 11? Write it down!

ARE YOU IMPACTED EASILY OR JUST ENTERTAINED?

Ask yourself, "are you looking to be impacted (having a strong effect on something or someone) or entertained (just distractions; provide someone with amusement or enjoyment for the moment).

Sometimes we are more excited about entertainment than about something that could be impactful. What could you be doing that could impact you, your family, your career, etc. Impact lasts for a lifetime. Being entertained lasts only for a short while. If you're on social media for hours getting wrapped up in other people's lives – there's no impact; it's merely entertainment.

Add up the hours spent on social media and texting. Add it up and see how long you were involved in entertainment versus impactful conversation. Most people you're watching on social media are getting paid to entertain you not to impact you.

FRANK'S STORY

I had just got kicked out of Mississippi junior college. My mom begged the coach in Mississippi not to send me home in fear that I would possibly die from getting back involved with crime and the wrong crowd. She asked him to send me somewhere else. So, he called a friend at a junior college in Kansas. Well, I got to Kansas Junior College, and I got in more trouble again. I got arrested for a shoot-out.

When I got out of jail and bonded out, I didn't even call for a ride. I was so happy for another opportunity; I walked all the way home. On that walk home, I talked to myself the whole way, and I realized the impact of the people in my life that told me the truth instead of entertaining my feelings. They didn't entertain my lust and my feelings; they impacted my heart by being honest with me and telling me that I was about to mess up my life. They told me I was going to wind up dead, that I was making mistakes, and I was doing wrong.

They impacted my life by being truthful, so that's what I want to share with you. You can find yourself in bad situations if you're following entertainment, and that's what I was doing. That's why I found myself incarcerated again, but if I would've followed the impact, I wouldn't have been in that situation at all.

You may not find yourself in a situation as critical as mine; incarcerated with charges and facing 10 to 15 years, but it could be something as simple as following the wrong person and getting pulled over and they got drugs in the car. You were so focused on entertaining or being entertained by this person, because they were cool, or because you thought they were a good person to be around because it entertained you. If you're going to be successful in life, if you're going to get the secret in life, you're going to have to stop being moved by entertainment and start being moved by impact.

Here's a question to ask yourself; and be very honest with yourself. This is very important because if you're not honest with yourself, you'll miss the whole point. Are you easily impacted. Do you impact or just entertain?

Impact means that you're impacted by truth, righteousness, and it's important to you to make sure that you fine tune yourself to be right. If it's entertainment that you're moved by, then it doesn't take much to get you going and it doesn't take much for you to believe a lie, because it sounds good.

Entertainment is the substitute for the joy that God promised you. The Bible says the joy of the Lord is your strength. It says nothing about entertainment.

REFLECT

Think about it.

What are you impacted by? What do you consider entertainment? *Look at the chart below and identify the actions that either entertain or impact you by marking them with an "X" under the appropriate column. Use the blank lines to add things you spend a lot of time doing and enter whether it "entertains" or "impacts" you.*

Action	This Action Entertains Me	This Action Impacts Me
Celebrity gossip on Instagram, Tik tok, etc.		
Gossiping, thinking and talking about past hurt.		
Texting friends all day long.		

TIME OUT WITH FRANK D. MURPHY: Impact makes you focus. Entertainment is a distraction.

A lot of people are distracted by entertainment. They are distracted while they're at school, at work, at the gym, on their commute, and even when they are out with family and friends. Have you replaced focusing on your life dreams and goals with TV, partying, and social media? A life focused on entertainment and distraction does not support growth. These individuals are stuck in jobs they hate, in meaningless relationships, and on a path going nowhere. Refocus your mind on being impacted and how you can impact others.

Refocus your Mind.

Be honest with yourself, are you distracted with social media, partying, misguided friends, etc.?

☐ **Yes** ☐ **No**

What do you need to change in your life to be impacted or make an impact? *Examples: Cut back the amount of time on social media; spend more time researching careers; or spend more time perfecting my craft.*

Take a piece of paper out and write down how you would like to impact your family and friends, your community, and the world. Tape the paper to your mirror so that you look at it repeatedly. Now go and start making impact.

Take action right **NOW!**

PLAY 12 WRAP UP

You must refocus your priorities and invest in yourself and your growth. It's simple — entertainment and distraction are the enemy of growth and success. They will make sure you stay mediocre or simply average.

Life is short so you don't have the luxury of waiting to make an impact. I know that learning, staying focused, and improving yourself may not be popular however it is for those who seek to be successful.

WHAT'S MY PLAN TO MASTER PLAY 12? Write it down!

YOU MUST KNOW THE DIFFERENCE BETWEEN A FAN AND A FRIEND

Knowing the difference between a fan versus a friend can help you avoid relationship issues. We all have people that come into our life for a reason, a season and sometimes for life. You must understand that not everyone that comes into your life is meant to stay.

A fan will sing your praises and cheer for you if you are winning. They also seek to get rather than give. They are driven by their selfish needs and desires. A friend has your best interest in mind and is genuinely seeking an authentic relationship. They are there to support you and aren't afraid to correct you if necessary.

You must be careful because a friend and a fan can sometimes look very similar. For example, there may be a man who doesn't live according to the culture, meaning he doesn't mistreat women, sleep around, degrade women, or he doesn't go out to the clubs all the time. Would a friend or a fan get upset because this man isn't doing what they do? Or perhaps there is a woman who use to hang out all the time however she started focusing on meeting someone. She meets someone and gets married then suddenly the friends she hung out with stop being her friend. They were her so called friends until she received her blessing of a lifelong companion. Are these women truly friends or fans? Even though she's now married, do they still want to be part of her life or are they simply jealous?

Who are the friends and fans in your life?

FRANK'S STORY

When I was first drafted, I always liked to come back to Jacksonville, Florida, my hometown to show love. I thought the guys I used to hang with were still my friends, but it's hard to be a friend when you're no longer on their level. I was no longer in the streets, and I didn't sell dope anymore. I had a real job in the NFL, and I was on TV every week during football season. I also had a lot of money, and it was legal.

Well, I kept going back to the fans. They were no longer my friends, they were fans, which means when you become a fan in a hood (a neighborhood), you're on the streets which means you can get robbed or put your life in jeopardy because they don't care because you're no longer doing the same thing they're doing.

I found myself going home and still hanging on the corner with these guys. One time, they got in an argument and just pulled out a gun and start shooting at this guy right in front of me, knowing I'm in the NFL and knowing I can't be around that stuff and things of that nature. They didn't even care how their actions could affect me. I had to recognize it, not them. So, in

play 13, you have to depend on yourself to recognize this is not a friend anymore, this a fan, because a friend would have never pulled out a gun and start shooting or put my life in jeopardy. With these boys shooting back, a bullet could have hit all of us. So, when you have stories like that, you can't let anybody live a fantasy through you. You see, fan is short for fantasy.

I have another short story to share with you. I remember playing for the Tampa Bay Buccaneers, I was standing back for a kickoff return. The crowd was so loud. They were cheering me on to catch this kick and run it back for a touchdown. I couldn't hear the stadium was so loud. But I noticed when I got hurt, there was another guy that had to go back and kick return because I was hurt. They were cheering just as loud for him, as they were for me. I realized that they were living a fantasy through me just as they were living a fantasy through him.

They didn't care who was back there to receive the ball, they found something to live a fantasy through. So, I'm telling you, don't let anybody live a fantasy through you. Make sure that they're your real friend and not living a fantasy through you.

So, I encourage you to check your circle.

FRANK'S CHALLENGE

To make sure you understand: A friend will be honest with you; a fan will tell you what you want to hear. A friend is going to correct you; a fan will agree with you no matter whether you're right or wrong. A friend will love you when you make a mistake, a fan will point out the mistake and throw it up in your face when it benefits them. So, I challenge you to make sure that your circle is full of friends not fans.

REFLECT

Take a look at how we defined a friend and a fan above. Now think about your inner circle. Which list do the individuals in your inner circle fall under. Are they all friends? Are any of them fans?

Think about it.

Recall a time when you were struggling or had a problem. How did your friends react?

Were they supportive? Negative? Or indifferent?

Now that you know the difference between a friend and a fan, as you meet potential friends to join your inner circle, you can evaluate them closely to determine whether they are really a friend or a fan.

Refocus your Mind.

Evaluate yourself. Are you a good friend? What makes you a good friend? *You listen to your friends. You're supportive when your friend is in need.*

TIME OUT WITH FRANK D. MURPHY: Relationships require give and take on both parties part. Keep in mind that you shouldn't be the only one giving. If you find that you are the only one committed to the relationship, then the other person may be taking advantage of you or perhaps they are simply just a fan.

Start investing your time in people who care about you and that you care about. And don't be afraid to end relationships with the fans in your life.

RESPOND!

Take action right
NOW!

PLAY 13 WRAP UP

Don't allow just anybody in your inner circle. Determine what you need in a friend and use that to determine the right friends for you.

WHAT'S MY PLAN TO MASTER PLAY 13? Write it down!

STOP COMPETING

You should always look for collaboration over competition. Stop comparing your talents with someone else's. You need to learn how to work together instead of competing with others. Be satisfied with your portion. Everyone else's gift may not be your gift. God is pleased when we put in the effort to be the best we can be.

People who are competitive feel undo pressures such as the pressure to be skinny to the point of anorexia; the pressure to be rich to the point where they will steal from a loved one; or the pressure to be the best at something to the point where you lose sleep at night and become depressed.

Sadly, some people need to watch another person lose in order to feel good about themselves. Some have to dominate or put someone else down in order to feel superior or worthy.

Look at social media where people are constantly body shaming, posting their material things to make others jealous, or posting their many achievements in order to make others feel they are inadequate. If you fall into the trap of competing, you will always feel like you don't measure up. It is better to collaborate with others. This way you work together to make each of you the best you can be.

FRANK'S STORY |

Every year, NFL hopefuls coming out of college hope to be chosen to showcase their talents in the All-Star game. I was chosen to showcase my talents which was a great opportunity because all the NFL Scouts and coaches were there.

I had a great showing in the All-star game as a running back. I scored a touchdown, caught the ball, ran the ball — I was doing good. I had a great quarter however you must switch time with other players so everyone gets seen.

It was the other running back's turn, so they brought me out and put him in. He fumbled the ball, and the other team got the ball and ran it back. The coach was furious. The coach said, "you're out, Frank, go back in." I went back in. If I had a competing spirit or was in a competing mindset, I would have just taken the game over and made sure the other guy never touched the field again. But instead, I remembered the look on the guy's face and decided I had to do something.

The guy knew he fumbled in front of the NFL scouts, and he thought there was no way he was going to get drafted. So, I got into the game and after the first run, I hopped off and told the coach that my legs were tight and that I was cramping. The coach told the guy to go back in. He stopped and we looked at each other and I just winked my eye at him.

He went in and played one of the better games. He ran touchdown after touchdown. He came back to the sideline and said, "Bro, I know you ain't hurt." I said, "No, man, but I'm not competing with you. I want to assist you; I want to give you an opportunity. I already had a good quarter. I already scored. The Scots are already loving me. I didn't want you to leave this game, not like that."

It turns out that because I assisted the guy, he told the NFL scouts the story and they looked at me totally differently then. They now thought that in addition to my talent, I was a good teammate. It boosted my draft opportunities and I needed that because I had all the felonies on my record and stuff like that. I needed anything positive that I could get to get drafted.

You must ask yourself, are you competing or are you assisting. Now, this does not mean you have to go around assisting everybody. I'm not telling you to go out here and assist the world. When it is time for you to assist the right person, you'll know.

When you see someone achieve a goal, human nature makes it so easy to feel jealous of them. It's important that you remember you don't know that person's story. You don't know their struggles and what they went through to reach their goal. You may be seeing them in a time of success, but you may not know the number of failures and the many hours they spent getting to this point.

Be happy for them, congratulate them on their success. You should admire their hard work and use their success as motivation. Do not turn them into your competition, rather get inspiration from them. Look at it in a positive way; if they can do it, then you can too.

REFLECT

Think about it.

Who are you secretly competing with? *Someone from school, a co-worker, your sibling, etc.*

How can you collaborate with them so you both can inspire each other?

Refocus your mind on collaborating! When you see other people as your competitors, it's hard to appreciate their good qualities. You will see them as someone to compete against, do better than, and forget that working with them can be beneficial for you and them.

Imagine how much you can learn from them. You could pick up a new skill, see a new perspective, or perhaps learn something new about yourself. You could also build a healthy relationship with someone with like interest. When you are open to learning from others, they can learn from you too.

Refocus your Mind.

Think about someone you secretly compete with. What are some of the qualities you could possibly learn from them if you collaborated with them?

Stop comparing yourself to others right now!

Keeping up with people on social media shouldn't be the motivation behind why you do things. Stressing over the number of likes you have will cause you to spend time, effort, and money for approval you don't need.

In Isaiah 43:1, the Lord promised us: "I have redeemed you; I have summoned you by name; you are mine." Comparison and competition will always be a struggle, but we must remember, we don't belong to other people who like our pictures or post. We belong to a God who *loves* us, and that should make you content.

Take action right **NOW!**

TIME OUT WITH FRANK D. MUR-PHY: Focus on the quality of your life instead of the quantity of your likes and comments on social media.

PLAY 14 WRAP UP

It can be easy to get caught up in the idea of competing with others. One thing to remember, there is always going to be someone that seems better or more capable than you so focus on you. Spend your time learning and growing into who you want to be so that your future self can be proud of the work you put in.

WHAT'S MY PLAN TO MASTER PLAY 14? Write it down!

THE RIGHT PLAYBOOK WILL HELP YOU DISCOVER YOUR PURPOSE

I've always felt like my purpose in life was to help people. To find your purpose, you must look back over your life and take a close look at your backlog (your life). The reason why you're going to look at your backlog, is that's how you're going to discover and know your purpose. If you look at your backlog, you'll discover things that you have always leaned towards. For example, how you had a passion for helping people without really noticing it, how you had a passion for teaching others, etc. If you look at your backlog, you'll see how you inspire people without really trying — it just came naturally.

For instance, in the NFL, I didn't know that I had influence over some of the players I played with. I wasn't a star player, and most players try to follow behind the star players on the team. It turns out that I had influence over many of the players because of who I was, how I talked, how I walked, and how I carried myself.

FRANK'S STORY

When I played for the Miami Dolphins, the night before the game we always had a hotel room to ourselves. I remember one game the hotel made a mistake and overbooked the hotel, so we had to room with someone. Now, I was mad—I'm not going to lie. I wanted a room by myself like normal. I wanted to daydream about what I was going to do in the game and all of that. To make matters worse, when I got to the room, the dude I was assigned to the room with, took the side of the room that I always get. So, I got even madder.

I was taking my stuff out of my bag, and I was still kind of upset, and then he kept looking at me. I thought to myself, "this dude keeps staring at me, something ain't right." I asked him, "hey man, you okay? You keep staring at me." He said, "how do you do it?" I said, "how do I do what?" He said, "man, I read an article about you, man, I've seen the stuff you do, and I see how people look at you in the locker room. They are always coming up to you asking you questions. Even the star players always asking you questions and you're not even a star player, but they talk to you like that." I said, "I don't know, I didn't notice it." He said, "I need your help Frank because I'm on Cocaine, could you please help me?"

I was like, whoa. All this time I was mad because I didn't have the room to myself, and God was doing a divine connection and relationship building. I ended up mentoring him and helping him change his life. It was almost a year later when his family ran up to me. His kids hugged my leg, and his wife hugged my neck. It was one of the best feelings.

That's why I tell people, you have to look at your backlog. It's going to help you discover and know your purpose every step of the way. Once you take a good look at your backlog, sometimes you will realize that you've been in your purpose all along. You just didn't know it or recognize it. Take a look at your life. How many people have you helped or how many things have you done naturally without even trying? It was just a part of your everyday movement or part of your everyday helping assignment. I promise, you will start knowing your purpose when you look at your backlog.

FRANK'S CHALLENGE

When you start realizing your purpose, don't just say it out loud, take a piece of paper out and write it down so you can look at it every day. I challenge you to read that paper every single day.

Passion is a burning desire that you can't stop thinking about. Something you think about all the time. Take the time to think about the things you are most passionate about. Is it singing? Sports? Art? Business?

As mentioned before, sometimes you have to take a look at your backlog (your past) and your passion will be revealed to you.

REFLECT

Think about it.

What do you have a passion for? If you could do three (3) things that do not require you to get paid, what would those three (3) things be? *Remember, these three (3) things are things you are most passionate about. One of these items, if not all of them, is your purpose.*

	I'm most passionate about….
1	
2	
3	

Do you believe that your passion(s) align with your purpose?

☐ Yes   ☐ No

In what ways can you change your life to begin to live in your purpose? *Change who you turn to for advice, change who you hang out with, change how you spend your spare time, etc.*

Take a piece of paper and write a list of the people you normally hang around. Now think about your relationship with each person. Write down how each person benefits you and how they fit in with your purpose.

REFOCUS!

RESET

Refocus your Mind.

Do the people you surround yourself with share the same passions you do or are they focused on things they are passionate about? *Do you share common interests? If not, are they motivated to follow their own passions?*

☐ Yes   ☐ No

Do the people you surround yourself with encourage you? *If you're a basketball player, do they come to your games and cheer for you? If you're studying, do they help you study or allow you quiet time to study without making you feel guilty?*

☐ Yes   ☐ No

Do the people you surround yourself with call you out when they see you are about to do something wrong or something that could alter your future?

☐ **Yes**   ☐ **No**

So, you've figured out what you're passionate about and the people that will most likely be on your support team as you pursue your purpose. Now write down the steps you will take to start pursuing your purpose. Remember to include seeking out a mentor to provide direction along the way. Also, select one or two individuals from your support team that you can depend on to hold you accountable. Make sure the individuals are your true supporters and not just fans.

Take action right **NOW!**

	The steps I will take to start pursuing my purpose are:
1.	*Example: I will cut my tv time down.*
2.	*Example: I will stop spending so much time on social media.*
3.	
4.	
5.	
6.	
7.	
8.	

TIME OUT WITH FRANK D. MURPHY: Your purpose is not just about you. Your purpose is to help others. If what you believe is your purpose hurts others in any way, then that is not your true purpose. For example, if you say your purpose is to be a rapper. That may be your purpose, but if your songs degrade women, talk about killing people or selling drugs, that's not your purpose because it hurts people. Your purpose may be to rap but not about things that hurt people. Make sure you don't have a false, fake or perverted purpose.

PLAY 15 WRAP UP

Colossians 3:3 "Your life is with Jesus but hidden in God." This scripture means you must be honest, you must believe in something greater than yourself. Go to the source of who created you. Finding your purpose starts with believing in something greater than yourself. This is how I identified my purpose, stay in my purpose and now I'm finishing my purpose.

WHAT'S MY PLAN TO MASTER PLAY 15? Write it down!

THE RIGHT PLAYBOOK WILL HELP YOU IDENTIFY THE VOICE OF YOUR HEART

Know the voice of your heart, not the voice of your experiences. Your head is not your heart. When you know the playbook, you'll make the right move. Trust your intuition. Time to time, you will hear a gentle, faint voice that's speaking to your heart and urging you to do, or perhaps not to do something. Listen to that voice. It will prevent you from making bad decisions, mistakes, or being somewhere or with someone you shouldn't. The small voice can help you reach your potential, and it can also keep you out of harm's way.

I know people hear this voice all the time in their heart, and this is the voice of the heart. Trust me, it will save your life; it'll save you from getting in bad relationships; and it will save you from getting in bad business deals.

FRANK'S STORY

When I was in Orlando, I was praying in my room and meditating, and suddenly I heard the voice of my heart say, pray for your teammates. But it wasn't just to pray for them, it told me to pray for them every morning. So, for the whole entire season, I got up every morning at 6am, way before everyone got in the stairways. I would go into the stairway and pray for all my teammates every morning. Nobody knew I did this because everyone would still be asleep. I prayed for them because the voice of my heart was telling me that people are hurting and they needed help, they need prayer, and they need guidance.

As you probably know, before we go out to play a game, we all come in the huddle to pray as a team. So, one day we were in the locker room, and everybody grabbed hands, and I put my head down. I really had never prayed before in front of them. I had never talked about God or anything. So, everybody put their head down. I happened to look up and everybody was looking at me and waiting for me to lead the prayer.

So that story registers with me a lot when I think about listening to the voice of your heart. At that moment, those guys were looking at me to pray, and I had never prayed in front of them before, but they knew it was me that was supposed to lead prayer. They were all looking at me because that's what happens when you hear the voice of the heart.

It's so important that you understand the concept of listening to the voice of your heart that I have a bonus story for you. I remember playing out with some friends and I'll never forget this moment. We all were sitting at the school waiting around for our rides. Well, our rides didn't come so we had to walk home. A couple of our friends said, "man we are going to walk ahead, are y'all gonna stay here?". I said, "you know what, I'm gonna go ahead and walk ahead with this group here". It turns out, the voice in my heart was repeatedly telling me that I needed to leave and to not stay back with the others. I kept hearing that you need to leave.

It wasn't no more than 30 minutes later, the other group got up and walked home cause their rides didn't come either. They ended up pulling some man out of a car, trying to carjack him and the man shot at them trying to kill all of them. And because I was with the other group, because the voice of my heart said go with this other group, we didn't know anything about it until it was over. We weren't even around.

So, the voice of your heart can save your life, the voice of your lust and greed will destroy your life and sometimes even end your life. If you want to be successful in life and in business, you must know the difference between the voice of your heart and the voice of your lust/greed.

TIME OUT WITH FRANK D. MURPHY: Listen to the voice of your heart, not the voice of your lust/greed. You must make a choice. Listen to your heart or your lust/greed. It's just one or the other.

I remember one night my head was telling me that I should go out. On the other hand, my heart said I should stay in. I listened to my heart that night. It turns out there was a shooting at the party I was going to go to. My experience is an example of how important it is not to be so headstrong that we are not moved by our hearts. Think about times when you listened to your heart, when you ignored your heart, or you wish you would have listened to your heart.

REFLECT

Think about it.

What is it your inner voice telling you to do or not to do? *For example, in your family, on your job, as far as your goals, etc.*

When it comes to decision-making, do you follow your head or your heart?

Do you respond right away when a problem occurs, or do you take a second to think and weigh your options first?

Are you still struggling to hear that inner voice? Perhaps you need to spend some quiet time getting to know that voice.

Refocus your Mind.

FRANK'S CHALLENGE

Find a quiet place – perhaps your room, in a park, or in your basement. Close your eyes and just breathe in and out slowly. Spend time meditating on a situation you're dealing with. Your small voice may not show up right at that moment but with a little practice and trusting your heart, it will show up right when you need it.

Write down a good decision and a bad decision you made in the last month or so. Ask yourself were those decisions made from the heart or from the head. *For example, I decided not to get in the car with a friend who had been drinking. That night they ended up getting in a serious accident.*

Start practicing today!

Start practicing recognizing the difference between a head or heart decision. This will take practice however you will be able to recognize that inner voice. Start realizing the difference between thinking with your head or your heart.

Take action right **NOW!**

TIME OUT WITH FRANK D. MURPHY: Getting to know the voice in your heart is just as important as knowing the voice of your friend, wife, coach, etc. You must become friends with the voice of your heart. That voice in your heart must become your best friend. This is the first step of your becoming successful in life. You must practice listening to it.

PLAY 16 WRAP UP

Do not allow your experiences to define your decision-making. When it is time to make decisions, allow your heart (gut feeling) and intuition to take the lead. Allow that small, faint voice to speak to your heart. It will save you from bad decisions and bad experiences.

WHAT'S MY PLAN TO MASTER PLAY 16? Write it down!

WHAT BARS ARE HOLDING YOU BACK FROM YOUR NEW PLAYBOOK?

I ask this question because these plays are constant questions to get you to be honest with yourself. If you can't be honest with yourself, it's going to be hard for you.

You don't have to be behind bars for something to hold you back. I was behind bars that were physically holding me back, but what is holding you back? What's your excuse for not being successful in doing the things you feel you need to do to be successful. So, when I say bars holding you back, is it your attitude? You don't have character? You're always lying? Your cheating? Those are bars. Are those bars holding you back from the real you and from you living your best life? If so, then you must figure out how to get that key and open that door.

One day, I figured out that the bars that were holding me back weren't prison bars. It was bars of who I kept around me (fake friends), fake brands (ie, what's popular, trends, statically, etc), bad habits, bad decisions, my attitude, etc. Those were bars. I had a lot of bars I had to get unlocked.

You need to look in your life and identify the bars that are holding you back. Do you have a grudge against somebody? Do you need to forgive somebody like your parents or a friend? You have to figure out what those bars are, or you will never reach your full potential.

FRANK'S STORY

At the age of 15, I was incarcerated. I'll never forget walking through the jail smelling the stinky socks and the stench in the air. I saw paint chipped walls just falling as I walked through. When they took me to my cell and they shut that door, I knew this wasn't the place for me. I knew I couldn't let these bars define me.

I had to mentally understand that I had to change this situation, and it's not going to change by itself, or because I'm saying it, or because somebody told me I had to change. The situation is in my mind and how I make decisions.

While I was incarcerated, I used to go to the window, it's a little peep hole window that you could see out. I used to stare out that window and look out and see the outside. I never looked at the bars because I was focused on the outside, even though it was a little peep hole. I would see cars passing by and I would talk to myself and say, I will have that type of car. I would see people walking freely and I would say to myself, I'm going to be free. I would see people laughing and playing out there, and I would say to myself, I'm going to be laughing and playing.

I was locked up, so I had to take a little peep hole and keep my eyes focused on what was outside. I turned my back on my bars, so I'm asking you to turn your back on your bars. Your bars are holding you back and it's time to refocus. Once I refocused, my mindset changed even while I was incarcerated, so if I can do it behind bars, I know that you can do it when you're free.

TIME OUT WITH FRANK D. MUR-PHY: One thing that I did, I had to keep my eyes off the bars. I encourage you to keep your eyes off the bars and find something to replace them with.

By allowing the bars to hold you back you are essentially holding your dream captive. If the bars are holding you back, you aren't taking the steps to confront your fears, release anxiety or stepping out on faith. Perhaps you are just used to living in your comfort zone that being behind bars feels safer.

You must first conquer what's holding you back – your mind.

REFLECT

Think about it.

Close your eyes and imagine yourself behind bars. When it comes to something holding you back from your dreams, what do those bars represent for you? *Do the bars represent fear of failure, lack of confidence in your talents or fear of acceptance, etc.*

What steps will you take to unlock your bars? *I'll talk to someone I trust.*

Once you recognize and write down the bars that are holding you back, I encourage you to keep your eyes off the bars and find something to replace them with. For example, if fear is holding you back, replace it with confidence. If your attitude is holding you back, then change your words. These are simple changes you can make. It may take some time to master the changes, however baby steps are better than no steps at all.

Refocus your Mind.

What's most important to you? *For example, becoming a rapper, becoming a model, opening a hair salon, or playing for the NFL or NBA, etc.*

What do I need to let go of and stop doing to spend more time working on what's most important to me? *Lazy friends, time spent on social media, bad habits like alcohol, overeating, drugs, etc.*

Some people let the bars hold them back simply by their inability to get out of their own way and take action! They get so overwhelmed by the thought of change (unlocking the bars), that they choose to do **NOTHING.**

So, if you're telling yourself that you **DO** really want that new job, to start your own business, or pursue your degree, then you have to **DO** something about it. You cannot sit back, and hope things just work out for you. You have to just **DO IT**.

RESPOND!

Take action right **NOW!**

TIME OUT WITH FRANK D. MUR-PHY: Faith without works is dead. They work hand-in-hand.

PLAY 17 WRAP UP

The bars that are holding you back can easily be open if you let go of your fears. Take the steps necessary to overcome your fears and watch how bright it is on the other side of your bars.

WHAT'S MY PLAN TO MASTER PLAY 17? Write it down!

THE NEW PLAYBOOK WILL HELP YOU LOOK AT YOUR MONEY AS A PERSON

If you mistreat your money, it will mistreat you. In order to take care of yourself and your family, trust me, you want this relationship to last. You have to treat money as if it is a human being. You respect it. When you spend money on things you don't need or throw money around, you're not showing your money the respect that it deserves.

Afterall, money is how you provide you and your family's daily needs – food, shelter, clothing, transportation, etc. Why would you disrespect the very thing that ensures you can provide all your needs? Just as we respect the human beings in our lives that provide for us why wouldn't you do the same for your money?

FRANK'S STORY

I became a millionaire at a very early age, in my 20s. When I first went into the NFL, I remember one day being in my condo and on the floor just sitting there knowing I couldn't pay one bill, because I didn't treat my money right. When you don't treat your money right, it's impossible for the money to get you the return that you want. It's just like if you treat a person wrong. No matter what, that person is gonna get tired. No matter whether it's 10 years, five years, a month later, they're going to eventually leave you.

So, I tell people, you must look at your money as a person and you have to treat your money like a person and treat it with respect. Put your money in the position to be successful. Just like you would your daughter, your son, your wife, your husband, your boyfriend, girlfriend or a relative.

I wasn't doing that with my money. I was taking advantage of my money. I was giving my money away freely. I invested in businesses that I didn't do my due diligence to investigate. I partied all night with my money, traveled on private jets with my money, and outright mistreated my money. After a while, my money left me.

I had to quickly learn the value of money. Once I did, I never went through that again.

You may be thinking that all sounds good but what does it really mean to respect money? Essentially it means that you appreciate what money has the ability to do for you. You also need to understand the power of your money and that it must be used and managed wisely. If managed properly, money can help you improve your life and the lives of others. It can also help you achieve your goals and dreams.

REFLECT

Think about it.

FRANK'S CHALLENGE

Don't squander your money away, trying to keep up with others. Think about some of the choices you've made with your money. What changes do you need to make to fully respect your money? One of the ways I challenge you, is to search social media for financial influencers that will help you better manage your money.

Do you consider yourself a good handler of money? *Do you blow through money, or do you always have a little bit set aside for emergencies?*

☐ **Yes**　　☐ **No**

If not, how can you change the way you view money so that your money will last.

One of the most important aspects of managing money is understanding the difference between wants and needs. It's important to know which parts of your monthly expenses are an absolute need, and which items would be nice to have, but are not really necessary.

Your needs include food, shelter, utilities, transportation costs, insurance, and basic clothing and tools you need for school or work. A want is anything you buy that you can comfortably live without and is not essential for survival. Wants include eating out, going to the movies, or buying the newest cell phone (when yours is working fine).

I'm not saying you can't enjoy items that are "wants" but if those items are causing you financial pain or the inability to have money set aside for emergencies or pursuing your dreams, then are they really that important? Start evaluating all of your purchases to ensure they are really necessary.

REFOCUS!

Refocus your Mind.

Make a list of items you buy every month. Do you really need every item on your list to live and function? *How different would your life be if certain items were not on your list?*

Do the items on your wants list bring value to your life?

☐ **Yes**   ☐ **No**

TIME OUT WITH FRANK D. MUR-PHY: Take charge of your finances now. Start by creating a budget. With a quick google or app search, you can find an easy budgeting tool that will quickly get you on your way to fully respecting your money. With a good spending plan, you'd be surprised at how much you can squeeze out of your income — no matter how big or small your paycheck.

Tracking your spending helps identify problem areas so you can start spending less on things you don't need and put that money towards something better like college, career training, or even paying cash for a reliable car.

Realize that life happens, and that emergency dental appointments, car problem, or job loss is going to happen. Budgets help make sure you always have extra funds for the unexpected.

RESPOND!

Take action right **NOW!**

Do you know how to track your money? *Below are a few apps that I've personally checked out. Take a look at each one and select the one that works best for you. We are not affiliated with any of these apps they are simply suggestions. It's a good idea to ask your friends if they have any recommendations or find a financial advisor.*

- Mint
- YNAB
- Goodbudget
- EveryDollar
- Personal Capital
- PocketGuard
- Honeydue
- Fudget

PLAY 18 WRAP UP

1 Timothy 6:10 says "For the love of money is the root of all evil." Not "money" itself, is the root of all evil, but "the love of money" is the root of all evil. Allow yourself not to fall in love with money. Instead, treat money in a way that your money will last forever.

WHAT'S MY PLAN TO MASTER PLAY 18? Write it down!

YOUR NEW PLAY BOOK REQUIRES COMMUNICATION

Lack of communication is one of the biggest reasons friends fight and even sometimes end their friendship. Things that aren't a big deal can sometimes get blown out of proportion simply because one person didn't properly communicate with someone else.

A lack of communication and/or listening skills is the biggest problem in communication. It is the cause of:

- Hurt feelings because a friend feels you aren't listening.
- Misunderstandings when something is not properly communicated.
- Arguments because someone doesn't allow the other person to fully communicate their feelings.

We should all learn how to openly communicate and actively listen. You should make sure you fully understand what someone is saying to you and ensure you are completely heard when there is an issue.

FRANK'S STORY

Years ago, I had a friend who stayed in the same condo as me. One day, I ran into the owner of the condos. We started to talk, and she said something that made me feel as though my friend had told the owner something I had told my friend in confidence. Note: assumption is the lowest form of knowledge.

I assumed based on some things she had said that he told her all my business. So out of anger, I began to tell her things about my friend because I felt like I had to defend myself. Instead of me going back to him and communicating, come to find out he didn't tell her anything. Unfortunately, she went back to my friend and told him about our conversation. All I had to do was communicate. The lack of a communication killed the relationship.

Playing without communication can cost you the game, relationships, business deals, etc. Just as lack of communication affected my friendship with a very good friend, it can really hurt you on the football field and in any other environment.

When I played for the Miami Dolphins, during one game, me and the quarterback were running a play and had a backup play. The quarterback never communicated the play and it cost us an interception. I ran one route, and the quarterback went another way. All we had to do was communicate in the huddle before you broke the huddle.

FRANK'S CHALLENGE

If you're not communicating you put yourself in the position to lose – lose friendships, relationships, business deals, etc. If you don't communicate, you're now assuming that the person knows how to handle you and your situation. Why leave it to chance, make sure you communicate.

Effective communication is the process of exchanging ideas, thoughts, opinions, knowledge, and data so that the message is received and understood with clarity and purpose. We know we are communicating effectively, if both the individual sending and receiving the message feels satisfied.

Take a self-evaluation. Are you an effective communicator? Do you speak in the right tone? Are you clear with your message? Do you have the right attitude when you communicate? Take some time to think about your communication skills.

REFLECT

Think about it.

TIME OUT WITH FRANK D. MURPHY: Assumption is the lowest form of knowledge. Never assume anything! That is why it is important to communicate so that you are successful in all relationships and situations.

Are you an effective communicator? *Does the person you're communicating with feel satisfied with your tone, attitude, and clarity when you communicate?*

How do you think social media has played a role in how you communicate? *I communicate more via social media or texting; I never talk to my friends face-to-face; or I sometimes later realize I misunderstood someone I communicated with via social media or text because we didn't speak in complete sentences.*

TIME OUT WITH FRANK D. MURPHY: Have you ever wondered why you have two ears and one mouth? It's because you have to listen to be successful in communicating with someone.

To become a more effective communicator you need to practice becoming a better listener. By that I mean that you need to practice giving your full attention when in a conversation.

Some techniques you should also practice include paying attention to your body language (waving arms and hands can be threatening), giving encouraging verbal cues (ie., good job, that's great, yes, etc.), and asking questions (this way you get clarity immediately if you didn't understand something the person said).

REFOCUS!

Refocus your Mind.

When you communicate, do you use body language? *For example, do you wave your arms or hands? Do you roll your eyes? Do you sigh?*

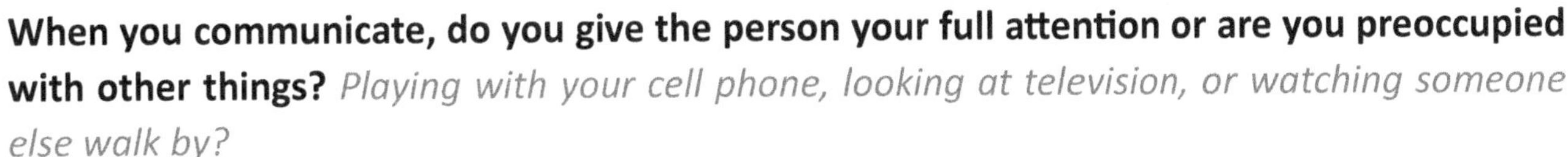

When you communicate, do you give the person your full attention or are you preoccupied with other things? *Playing with your cell phone, looking at television, or watching someone else walk by?*

How can you improve your techniques for effective communication?

Don't wait to put the communication skills we talked about in place. Think about how much better your conversations will be if you start practicing them immediately.

Sometimes people fail to understand that communication is key to getting things done. When done right, a lot can be achieved, and your message will be well received.

RESPOND!

Take action right
NOW!

TIME OUT WITH FRANK D. MURPHY: Here are 3 key points about communication:

1). Communicate to listen and try not to solve every problem.
2). Make sure you word your questions right and that you are respectful because your question can trigger a negative reaction and make the person defensive.
3). Watch your tone and facial expressions.

PLAY 19 WRAP UP

Each of us has probably, without realizing it, been guilty of poor communication. For the sake of our relationships—whether business, social, family, or intimate—we all need to practice our communication skills. If you don't, your poor communication skills can potentially lead to misunderstandings and arguments or worse, the loss of a very good relationship.

WHAT'S MY PLAN TO MASTER PLAY 19? Write it down!

USING YOUR NEW PLAYBOOK TO FIND YOUR POTENTIAL

Potential can be a deadly word. Potential is just potential until you do something. Some people hold on to "potential" for 10 years because it "feels good." Potential is what you CAN do, but you haven't done it yet.

In the dictionary, potential is defined as "having or showing the capacity to become or develop into something in the future". In simple terms, it's what you have the natural ability to do with your life.

I know understanding your potential seems hard but if you've really been paying attention to this workbook then realizing your potential really isn't that hard. It requires you to listen to that inner voice, look in your backlog, and to build your platform (character).

FRANK'S STORY

From a very young age I knew I wanted to play in the NFL. I didn't get to the NFL until I was 21, however even at the age of 9, I knew I had the potential.

I had to wait 12 years to reach my full potential and really get paid. Until football became my occupation, I had to do it for free with no guarantee that I was going to make it. Or no guarantee I was going to be drafted. I had to put in 12 years of hard work.

Because I knew I had potential, I meditated and prayed over my desire regularly. I was faithful to practicing, working out, and pursuing my dream as if it was already done. What I mean by that is I had faith that God had already answered my prayer. I woke up each day as if my dream had already been answered, however I simply hadn't seen or experienced my dreams yet. All I had to do was put a plan together until my dream was realized.

I planned out how much I should work out. How much I should run every day. What I needed to do to get better. I put the plan together, and then I prepared myself and my body for this opportunity for 12 years.

I didn't just sit around and do nothing. Are you preparing for your potential?

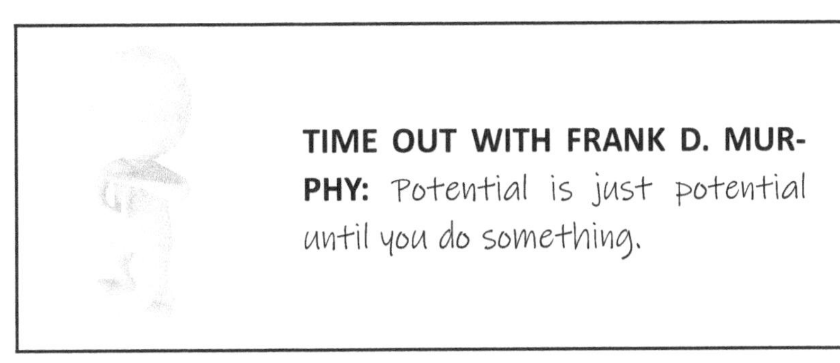
TIME OUT WITH FRANK D. MUR-PHY: Potential is just potential until you do something.

Part of reaching your full potential is understanding what the big picture looks like to you. In other words, what are the goals that you want to accomplish? When it comes to reaching your potential, it's important that you know what the big picture looks like.

Why do you do what you do? Think about it.

Think about it.

What is the big picture for you? *Write down your dreams, goals, or plans.*

Are you pursuing your potential every day? *Do you have a plan? Do you work on your plan a little bit every day?*

You have to set yourself up for success, not for failure. Each week you should create a to-do list of tasks that you want to accomplish that week.

Good time management and planning contribute to your success and reaching your fullest potential.

Refocus your Mind.

Do you make the best use of your time? *Can you carve out more time to pursue your dreams?*

☐ **Yes**   ☐ **No**

If you answered no, then what changes do you need to make to manage your time more effectively? *Spend less time in social settings, spend less time watching Netflix or AppleTV, etc.*

If you get distracted by your phone, the television, or friends who don't understand your agenda, you won't get things done. Make sure you put your phone on silent when you're trying to finish a task. Don't even touch or look at your television remote. And be sure to explain to your true friends what you're trying to achieve, I'm certain they will support you and understand when you can't hang out.

If you are disciplined and stay focused, trust me you will reap the rewards of your hard work.

Take action right **NOW!**

TIME OUT WITH FRANK D. MURPHY: Don't get distracted! It's easy to get off track and not get anything done. You have to be disciplined and stay focused on what you need to get done to reach your fullest potential.

PLAY 20 WRAP UP

Simply living each day pursuing your potential will be a great reward within itself. One day you'll look back over your life and realize that all the pain, sweat, and tears were worth the reward of reaching your highest potential.

WHAT IS MY PLAN TO MASTER PLAY 20: Write it down!

WILL YOU LEAVE BEHIND A LEGACY OR A CURSE?

There are two sure things you can leave to your kids — your legacy or your curse. The short definition of legacy is something that is passed on. In fact, a person's legacy can come in many forms. It could be someone's faith, ethics, or values; or from a financial perspective it could be their money or assets; it could be their reputation or character; or it could even be bad debt or generational curses.

What is the legacy you're leaving your loved ones? Your good and bad decisions affect the legacy or curse your loved ones could inherit. For this reason, we should consider our loved ones when creating our legacy. It's important to remember your legacy guides someone else's future.

FRANK'S STORY

Whatever role you play, someone is going to model you. No matter whether you're a rapper, movie star, football player, teacher, hair stylist, or salesclerk, there is someone that is watching you and wants to be exactly like you.

Yes, I was in the NFL, however in my younger days, I didn't do the things that would build a positive legacy for my family. In fact, my younger brother grew up looking up to me and even tried to copy everything I did. When he got old enough, I started taking him to clubs and introduced him to women and alcohol. Back then, I didn't know any better, so I didn't realize I was leaving a curse to someone I cared about so dearly. Back then, I was a bad role model and I introduced him to a lifestyle and culture that harmed him, and eventually he became an alcoholic.

I started to recognize how much my lifestyle affected his life, so I talked to him and tried to change the perception he had of me. I had to replace his current perception with legacy which meant no smoking, no drinking, no clubs, and no women. It was up to me to replace the curse with legacy actions.

You have to be careful because you never know who's watching you. Even if you're not a celebrity, athlete, or in places of high exposure, we each play a role, and somebody is going to model it. Especially when you have kids.

Now that you understand that you are potentially a role model to someone or maybe many people, you need to evaluate yourself again.

This time you need to think about how you live your life. You need to determine if you're living a life that makes you fit to be a positive role model that will leave a legacy for your loved ones; or are you living in a way that will potentially leave behind a curse to your loved ones? The choice is up to you.

Think about it.

What would your loved ones say you're leaving behind? A legacy or a curse? Why would they say either?

How do the younger people in your life view you? *They view me as a good source for advice and a motivator OR they don't like to spend much time with me and they would say I have a bad attitude.*

If their view is negative, is that the way you want them to view you?

□ Yes   □ No

If you said No, what do you need to do to change their view of you?

TIME OUT WITH FRANK D. MURPHY: Think about becoming a more positive role model for others. The first thing you should do is think about the areas in which you can change and focus on improving yourself.

Improving yourself becomes easier when you seek out your own positive role models to look up to. Consider who the role models are in your life and identify the characteristics they possess that you admire or would like to emulate. Trust me, in time, their legacy will rub off on you.

REFOCUS!

Refocus your Mind.

What are the qualities or characteristics that your ideal role model should have? *For exam-ple, kindness, a motivator, the ability to lead, etc.*

Of the people you are regularly around, who would you consider to model or emulate? *Your parent(s), your coach, your pastor, a successful friend, your boss, etc.*

PLAY 21 WRAP UP

People's perception of you is always developed by the way you carry yourself. Whenever you walk into any room, remember that the way you carry yourself always leaves a good or bad impression.

Also remember that there's always somebody watching you. Be sure to always be focused on the legacy you need to leave behind.

WHAT IS MY PLAN TO MASTER PLAY 21? Write it down!

SECRET PLAY NOTES! Write it down!

SKILLS FOR LIFE CURRICULUM

A FRANK D. MURPHY PROJECT

Frank D. Murphy left behind drugs, guns and jail to win the Heisman Trophy in Junior College and play for the Tampa Bay Buccaneers and three other NFL teams. Since starting MWP in 2009, Frank has poured into the community by supporting empowerment programs for youth. His efforts have been well recognized; he has been awarded the JTEP Hero Award, the Hero Award by the NHL Tampa Bay Lightning, the Most Valuable Philanthropist in Sports Award, and has even been a recipient of an Honorary Doctorate Degree in Humanitarianism and the Presidential Lifetime Achievement Award presented by former President Barack Obama. From NFL draft pick to founder and president of Mentoring with Purpose Charity, Frank D. Murphy is a true paragon of what a second chance really is. Battling incredible obstacles, tenacity and determination prevailed and his passion to help others realize their potential and become impactful leaders in their communities flourished.

Frank D. Murphy is the Author of "The Man Behind the Helmet - God of Second Chance", as well as the writer and Director of the educational stage play "The Man Behind the Helmet - The Life Story of Frank D. Murphy". He founded the "Put Down your Fake ID" conferences for youth and schools and created the Frank D. Murphy online Life Skills curriculum program. Frank is the first professional athlete to produce and write his own educational stage play derived from his book and create a digital life skills program. He not only gives insight into his challenges, but he also offers firsthand solutions. Frank is also writing and producing his first motion picture!

Frank's life story journeys from childhood to adulthood as he overcame the struggles of growing up in an at-risk, inner-city neighborhood. From guns to selling drugs to jail, it seemed the odds were stacked against

Frank while he faced the possibility of spending life behind bars. After given a second chance through NFL Superbowl Coach, Tony Dungy, Frank instantly goes from drugs, guns and jail to a star athlete and successful NFL player. Concluding a successful football career receiving countless awards such as the All-American, All State and Player of the Year award, Frank didn't stop there.

Since starting his foundation in 2009, Murphy consistently pours into his community supporting empowerment programs for the youth. Today, Frank is a national motivational speaker and has served as life coach and mentor to over 100,000 youth.